Workshop on Computational Semantics in Clinical Text

(CSCT 2013)

Held at the 10th International Conference on Computational Semantics (IWCS 2013)

Potsdam, Germany
19 March 2013

ISBN: 978-1-62748-398-8

Printed from e-media with permission by:

Curran Associates, Inc.
57 Morehouse Lane
Red Hook, NY 12571

Printed by Curran Associates, Inc. (2013)

For permission requests, please contact the Association for Computational Linguistics at the address below.

Association for Computational Linguistics
209 N. Eighth Street
Stroudsburg, Pennsylvania 18360

Phone: 1-570-476-8006
Fax: 1-570-476-0860

acl@aclweb.org

Additional copies of this publication are available from:

Curran Associates, Inc.
57 Morehouse Lane
Red Hook, NY 12571 USA
Phone: 845-758-0400
Fax: 845-758-2634
Email: curran@proceedings.com
Web: www.proceedings.com

TABLE OF CONTENTS

A Framework to Generate Sets of Terms from Large Scale Medical Vocabularies for Natural Language Processing

Salah Aït-Mokhtar Caroline Hagège Pajolma Rupi
Xerox Research Centre Europe*
Firstname.Lastname@xrce.xerox.com

Abstract

In this paper we present our ongoing work on integrating large-scale terminological information into NLP tools. We focus on the problem of selecting and generating a set of suitable terms from the resources, based on deletion, modification and addition rules. We propose a general framework in which the raw data of the resources are first loaded into a knowledge base (KB). The selection and generation rules are then defined in a declarative way using query templates in the query language of the KB system. We illustrate the use of this framework to select and generate term sets from a UMLS dataset.

1 Introduction

Information extraction from free medical text using Natural Language Processing (NLP) is currently an important field considering the huge and still growing amount of unstructured textual documents in the medical domain (patient data, clinical trials and guidelines, medical literature). The ability to process automatically the information expressed in these documents can help to bridge gaps between patient information and clinical literature and it can be an asset for a wide range of applications in medical Information Extraction (IE) and NLP. The first step for effective processing of medical free text is the recognition of medical terms[1] appearing in these documents. For better interoperability, this annotation should be as compatible as possible with reference vocabularies and ontologies of the domain. Nonetheless, the terms from such resources require filtering and transformation before they are integrated into annotation tools.

In this paper we present our work on the process of selecting the set of terms to be integrated in the NLP component. We will briefly review the state of the art, and then describe the framework we developed for declarative and easily-maintainable selection and adaptation of term sets, based on a knowledge base (KB) system and query language. We will illustrate the use of this framework to select and generate term sets from an initial UMLS dataset.

2 Related Work

Several tools for annotating terms in medical text are currently available. MetaMap (Aronson and Lang (2010)) uses the Metathesaurus information in the Unified Medical Language System (UMLS) (Bodenreider et al. (2004) and Bodenreider (2007)) in order to automatically determine the medical concepts referred to in text. MetaMap relies on the SPECIALIST Lexicon of UMLS (NLM (2009); Browne et al. (2000)), a general English lexicon which includes both medical terms and general domain lexical entries. cTAKES (Savova et al. (2010)) performs information extraction from clinical narratives. It consists

*This work has been done in the context of the European FP7-ICT EURECA project: http://eurecaproject.eu/.

[1]Throughout this paper, we use the word "term" to refer to any character string that denotes a medical concept or entity, except in the figure depicting the UMLS ontology model (figure 1) where "Term" has the UMLS term class meaning.

of sequential components contributing to an incremental and cumulative annotation dataset. MedKAT (Medical Knowledge Analysis Tool)[2] is an NLP tool dedicated to the medical/pathology domain. It consists of a set of modules which annotate unstructured data such as pathology reports, clinical notes, discharge summaries and medical literature. These annotation tools use UMLS, BioPortal[3] or in-house built vocabularies as sources for the building of medical lexicons. Harkema et al. (2004) proposed a large scale terminology system for storing terms, which are compiled into finite-state lexicons to perform term lookup in texts. For that goal, they set up a relational database where terms from different origins are kept. This approach has the advantage of centralizing all the terminological information one may want to use for different applications. The terms stored in the database are then extracted and compiled into finite state lexicons. However, the work did not cover the issue of filtering and transforming the original set of terms before their inclusion into the NLP component.

Because of the size and the variety of existing medical vocabularies and medical texts, the ability to select and adapt the terminological information can help improve effective NLP tools, as reported by Demner-Fushman et al. (2010). Hettne et al. (2010) and Wu et al. (2012) have also shown that term filtering operations are useful in building an adequate medical lexicon. Hettne et al. (2010) conducted experiments for the building of a medical lexicon using UMLS Metathesaurus. They use term suppression and term rewriting techniques to filter out or discard terms which are considered irrelevant. As a result, a new, more consolidated medical lexicon is produced for medical concept annotation. In Wu et al. (2012) the UMLS Metathesaurus terms characteristics are exploited for discovering which of them are generalizable across data sources. After a corpus study, they came out with a set of filtering rules that significantly reduced the size of the original Metathesaurus lexicon.

In order to implement these selections and adaptations of term sets from existing medical vocabularies in a declarative and easily-maintainable way, we propose a framework based on an ontological representation and on knowledge-base query templates that define selection and adaptation rules.

3 A general framework for generating medical lexical resources

In the general framework we propose, an ontological schema is defined to capture the information contained in the terminological resources, according to which the raw data of resources are imported and loaded into an efficient knowledge base (KB) system in the form of entities and relations (RDF-like triples/quads). Depending on the requirements of the foreseen NLP-based application, the user defines the set of terms to generate from the terminological KB by writing a set of query templates in the query language of the KB system. Each query template can be tagged as a **deletion**, **modification** or **addition**.

Deletion query templates contain a predefined unbound variable T that can be instantiated with a term from the KB: if the resulting query runs successfully, then the term should be deleted from the final output term set. Similarly, modification and addition query templates have two unbound variable T and NT: when variable T is instantiated with a term from the KB and the resulting query succeeds, variable NT is instantiated. The resulting values of NT are new terms that should replace the original term T in the case of modification queries, or should be added along with the original term to the output term set. The user provides the set of query templates as parameters to the term selection and generation engine. The engine iterates through all the terms of the KB: for each term, it instantiates the input variable T of each query template with the term. Deletion queries are tested first: if one of them succeeds for the current term, then the term is discarded from the output term set and the engine goes to the next KB term. If not, and if one of the modification queries succeeds for the term, then the engine adds the output value of the query (i.e. all possible values of variable NT) to the output term set. Finally, if one of the addition rule succeeds, then it adds both the original KB term and the output terms (i.e. all possible values of variable NT) to the output set. A new term is always assigned all the information of the original term from which it is produced (i.e. same concept(s), semantic type(s), etc.), together with a specific tag.

[2] `http://ohnlp.sourceforge.net/MedKATp/`
[3] `http://bioportal.bioontology.org/`

We use an in-house KB system, called SKB, to store all the data, and its query language to define the query templates. An example of a deletion rule is: discard any term that has more than 6 tokens (see section 4.3.2). It can be defined with the following query making use of a regular expression:

```
regex(T "(\S+\s){6,}\S+")
```

A more interesting case is the "semantic type" modification rule (see table 2, section 4.3.2), which removes any semantic type within parentheses inside the initial term: in the following query template, the $regex$ part captures the semantic type substring (captured group \2), checks that it's the name of a KB node n that represents a UMLS semantic type (i.e. has the "hasTreeNumber" property), and instantiates output variable NT by deleting that substring (and the parentheses) from the initial term T, and finally checks that the new term NT is not already assigned to the same concept c in the initial UMLS data:

```
regex(T ".*?( *\(([^\)]+)\) *).+") & n=@findEntity(\2) & umls:hasTreeNumber(n ?)
& NT=@replace(T " *\(([^\)]+)\)" "") & umls:hasName(c T) & ~umls:hasName(c NT)
```

By using such a KB storage and query language, the system we propose has the advantage of providing a clean, modular and declarative way to define, maintain and change the criteria of selecting and generating terms from large-scale terminological resources. There is no need to code the transformation and selection rules in a programming language. The only requirements are that: (a) the original terminological resource is loaded into a KB (this is done once), and (b) the query language of the KB system has to be powerful enough to make it possible to use regular expression matching and back references, and string related functions and operators (e.g. concatenation, length, replacement) inside the queries. As a matter of fact, we did not choose a relational DBMS and SQL to implement the system because some of the relevant selection and transformation rules cannot be implemented with single SQL queries.

4 An example: Extracting UMLS information for NLP tools

4.1 UMLS dataset

We use UMLS as the basis for the creation of medical lexicons. UMLS combines a variety of source vocabularies, ontologies and terminologies. Integration of over 100 sources generates a very large medical knowledge base. In our work, we use all the English terms of category 0 of the 2012AA release of UMLS (i.e. licence-free vocabularies). The subset consists of 46 different vocabularies and contains 3.97 million English terms referring to 1.9 million concepts.

4.2 Defining an ontology and loading UMLS data to the KB system

We want to provide declarative ways to specify criteria for terms and concepts that are relevant for the medical lexicon we aim to build. These criteria may include meta-information such as the source name or the category of the source, but also a selection by language, semantic types or linguistic characteristics of the term. We define an ontology model (see figure 1) that incorporates the **complete** knowledge about concepts, terms, semantic types and relations, contained in the UMLS Metathesaurus and Semantic Network. The aim of building this ontology is to have easily traversable structured information.

We developed a Perl program which parses the main UMLS files, extracts the information according to the ontology model and transforms it into a triples/quads that are loaded into the KB. We produced 139.7 million of triples for category 0 data (all languages. The data is then loaded into the KB, where it can be further explored before being compiled into finite-state lexicon.

4.3 Transformation of the set of medical terms

We exclude terms from the initial dataset on the basis of semantic types. We also take advantage of previously published work (Hettne et al. (2010); Wu et al. (2012)) to select the most useful cleaning

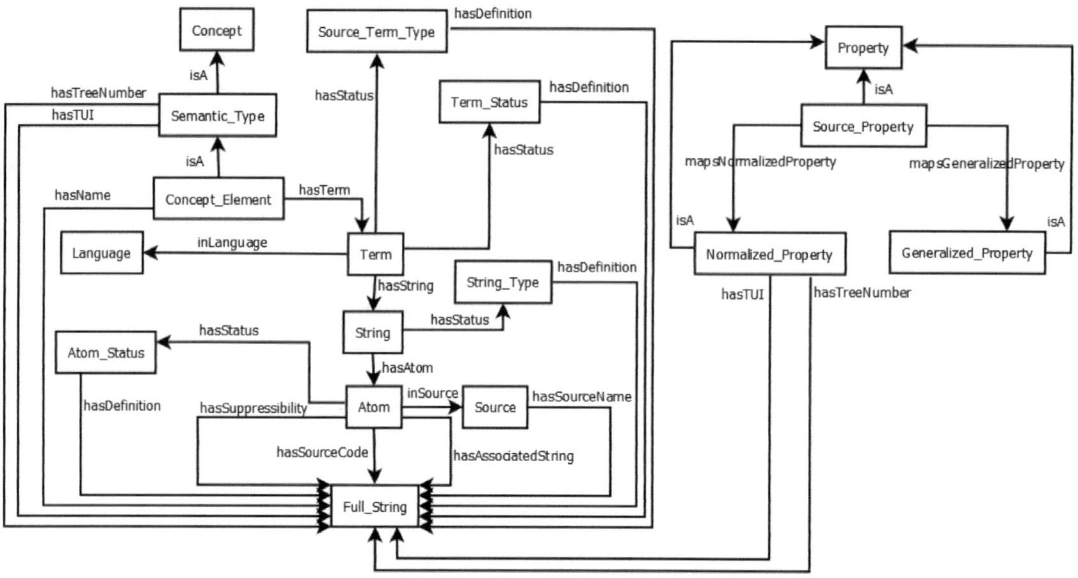

Figure 1: Ontology model

and transformation rules, and implement them with a few changes motivated by linguistic observation and experiments with the data. We compile the resulting terms with their UMLS semantic types into a finite-state transducer (FST), which is then unioned with the general lexical FST of the NLP components.

4.3.1 Cleaning by semantic types

Because we integrate the medical terms into a larger NLP system, we do not keep general domain information (i.e. information not specific to the medical domain). We discard terms belonging exclusively to UMLS concepts that have generic semantic types, e.g. semantic types corresponding to classical named entity types (like Organization and Geographic Area): the linguistic tools we rely on include a named entity recognition system that already captures this information in a more systematic way.

4.3.2 Transformation rules from the state of the art

We implemented term filtering rules described in Hettne et al. (2010) and Wu et al. (2012), using KB query templates described in 3. There are three main types of rules: deletion, addition and modification rules. The effect of each rule on the initial dataset is presented in tables 1, 2 and 3.

Table 1: Impact of deletion rules: number of deleted terms per rule

Rule	# deleted	Ex. of deleted term
Short token	893	*"9394"*
Dosages	388,019	*"Ampicillin 10g injection"*
At-sign	249,381	*"Medical and Surgical @ Muscles @ Transfer"*
EC	195	*"EC 1.1.1.62"*
Any classification	3,948	*"Unclassified ultrastructural features"*
Any underspecification	1,302	*"Unspecified amblyopia"*
Miscellaneous	9,625	*"Other causes of encephalitis"*
Special characters	45	*"[M]Brenner tumors (morphologic abnormality)"*
Maximum number of words	847,136	*Any term with 7 or more tokens*
Maximum number of characters	787,788	*Any term with more than 55 characters*

Table 2: Impact of modification rules: number of affected terms and number of resulting terms per rule

Rule	# matches	# resulting terms	Ex. impacted term	Ex. new term
Angular brackets	2,666	1,620	*"Bacteria <prokaryote>"*	*"Bacteria"*
Semantic type	419	411	*"Insulin (human) extract"*	*"Insulin extract"*

Table 3: Impact of addition rules: number of matching terms and number of new terms per rule

Rule	#matches	#new	Ex. matching term	Ex. output term(s)
Syntax inversion	494,518	482,236	*"GIST, malignant"*	*"malignant GIST"*
Possessives	7,263	7,263	*"Addison's Disease"*	*"Addison Disease"*
Short/long form	32,351	32,129	*"AD - Alzheimer's disease"*	*"AD", "Alzheimer's disease"*

4.3.3 Discussion of the transformation rules

Some of the filtering criteria adopted from Hettne et al. (2010) and Wu et al. (2012) have been slightly modified. We changed the ***Short token*** original rule to avoid filtering out relevant terms containing only one letter, like "*B*" (i.e. *Boron*, concept C0006030), or "*C*" (i.e. *Catechin*, concept C0007404). The ***Short form/long form*** (acronym/full term) original rule proposed by Hettne et al. (2010) used the algorithm in Schwartz and Hearst (2003). However, we found many cases not covered by the proposed algorithm, because the acronyms are not always built strictly from the first upper-case letters of the tokens of the terms tokens: e.g. "Cardiovascular Disease (CVD)", "Von Hippel-Lindau Syndrome (VHL)". Besides, there are UMLS terms in which the short form is at the beginning of the term. For example: "AD - Alzheimer's disease", "ALS - Amyotrophic lateral sclerosis", "BDR - Background diabetic retinopathy". We adapted the **short form/long form** rule accordingly.

5 Conclusion

We presented a framework for selecting and modifying large amounts of medical terms and integrating them into NLP lexicons[4]. Terms are first extracted from existing medical vocabularies present in the UMLS and stored into a knowledge base which preserves the original information associated to these terms (ontological and relational information). The way we store this information is in line with current trends of the semantic web and linked data. We took advantage of the powerful query language of a KB system in order to define filtering, suppression and transformation operations on the original terms. The most important characteristic of the approach is that this is performed in a declarative way, even for operations such as term modification. Consequently, the creation of new medical vocabularies for different NLP applications is easier than with programming-based methods. Finally, finite-state transducers containing these extracted and modified terms are first created and then combined with general purpose lexicons. The next stage will be to use and evaluate NLP tools relying on these lexicons.

References

Aronson, A. R. and F.-M. Lang (2010). An overview of MetaMap: historical perspective and recent advances. *JAMIA 17*(3), 229–236.

Bodenreider, O. (2007). The Unified Medical Language System (UMLS) and the Semantic Web. "`http://www.nettab.org/2007/slides/Tutorial_Bodenreider.pdf`".

[4]The system is licensable to clinical NLP community members.

Bodenreider, O., J. Willis, and W. Hole (2004). The unified medical language system. http://www.nlm.nih.gov/research/umls/presentations/2004-medinfo_tut.pdf.

Browne, A. C., A. T. McCray, and S. Srinivasan (2000). *The SPECIALIST LEXICON.* Lister Hill National Center for Biomedical Communications, National Library of Medicine.

Demner-Fushman, D., J. G. Mork, S. E. Shooshan, and A. R. Aronson (2010, August). UMLS content views appropriate for NLP processing of the biomedical literature vs. clinical text. *Journal of Biomedical Informatics 43*(4), 587–594.

Harkema, H., R. Gaizauskas, M. Hepple, A. Roberts, I. Roberts, N. Davis, and Y. Guo (2004, May). A large scale terminology resource for biomedical text processing. In *Proceedings of the NAACL/HLT 2004 Workshop on Linking Biological Literature, Ontologies and Databases: Tools for Users*, Boston.

Hettne, K., E. van Mulligen, M. Schuemie, B. Schijvenaars, and J. Kors (2010). Rewriting and suppressing UMLS terms for improved biomedical term identification. *Journal of Biomedical Semantics 1*(1), 5.

NLM (2009). SPECIALIST Lexicon and Lexical Tools. National Library of Medicine, National Institutes of Health, Bethesda, MD 20894, USA. http://www.ncbi.nlm.nih.gov/books/NBK9680/.

Savova, G. K., J. J. Masanz, P. V. Ogren, J. Zheng, S. Sohn, K. C. Kipper-Schuler, and C. G. Chute (2010). Mayo clinical text analysis and knowledge extraction system (cTAKES): architecture, component evaluation and applications. *Journal of the American Medical Informatics Association 17*(5), 507–513.

Schwartz, A. S. and M. A. Hearst (2003). A simple algorithm for identifying abbreviation definitions in biomedical text. In *Proceedings of the Pacific Symposium on Biocomputing*, pp. 451–462.

Wu, S. T.-I., H. Liu, D. Li, C. Tao, M. A. Musen, C. G. Chute, and N. H. Shah (2012). Unified Medical Language System term occurrences in clinical notes: a large-scale corpus analysis. *Journal of the American Medical Informatics Association 19*(e1), e149–e156.

Investigating Topic Modelling for Therapy Dialogue Analysis

Christine Howes, Matthew Purver and Rose McCabe
Queen Mary University of London
c.howes@qmul.ac.uk

Abstract

Previous research shows that aspects of doctor-patient communication in therapy can predict patient symptoms, satisfaction and future adherence to treatment (a significant problem with conditions such as schizophrenia). However, automatic prediction has so far shown success only when based on low-level lexical features, and it is unclear how well these can generalise to new data, or whether their effectiveness is due to their capturing aspects of style, structure or content. Here, we examine the use of *topic* as a higher-level measure of content, more likely to generalise and to have more explanatory power. Investigations show that while topics predict some important factors such as patient satisfaction and ratings of therapy quality, they lack the full predictive power of lower-level features. For some factors, unsupervised methods produce models comparable to manual annotation.

1 Introduction and Background

1.1 Therapy communication and outcomes

Aspects of doctor-patient communication have been shown to be associated with patient outcomes, in particular patient satisfaction, treatment adherence and health status (Ong et al., 1995). For patients with schizophrenia, non-adherence to treatment is a significant problem, with non-adherent patients having an average risk of relapse that is 3.7 times higher than adherent patients (Fenton et al., 1997). Some recent work suggests that a critical factor is conversation structure – *how* the communication proceeds. In consultations between out-patients with schizophrenia and their psychiatrists, McCabe et al. (tion) showed that patients who used more *other repair* — i.e. clarified what the doctor was saying — were more likely to adhere to their treatment six months later. However, outcomes are also affected by the content of the conversation – *what* is talked about. Using conversation analytic techniques, McCabe et al. (2002) show that doctors and patients have different agendas, made manifest in the topics that they talk about; on the same data, with topics annotated by hand, Hermann et al. (in prep) showed that patients attempt to talk about psychotic symptoms, but doctors focus more on medication issues. Importantly, more talk about medication from the patient increases the patient's chances of relapse in the six months following the consultation (Hermann et al., in prep).

1.2 Automatic prediction

Using machine learning techniques, Howes et al. (2012a,b) investigated whether outcomes such as adherence, evaluations of the consultation and symptoms can be predicted from therapy transcripts using features which can be extracted automatically. Their findings indicate that high-level features of the dialogue *structure* (backchannels, overlap etc) do not predict these outcomes to any degree of accuracy. However, by using all words spoken by patients as unigram lexical features, and selecting a subset based on correlation with outcomes over the training set, they were able to predict outcomes to reasonable degrees of accuracy (c. 70% for future adherence to treatment – see Howes et al., 2012a, for details).

These studies show that some aspects of therapy consultations which can be extracted automatically (thus removing the need for expert annotation) can enable accurate prediction of outcomes. However, as the successful features encode specific words spoken by the patient, it is unclear whether they relate to dialogue structure or content, or some combination of the two, and thus help little in explaining the results or providing feedback to help improve therapy effectiveness. It is also unclear how generalisable such results are to larger datasets or different settings, given such specific features with a small dataset. More general models or features may therefore be required.

In this paper, we examine the role and extraction of *topic*. Topic provides a measure of content more general than lexical word features; by examining its predictive power, we hope to provide generalisable models while also shedding more light on the role of content vs structure. As content is known to be predictive of outcomes to some extent, identification and tracking of topics covered can provide useful information for clinicians, enabling them to better direct their discussions in time restricted consultations, and aid the identification of patients who may subsequently be at risk of relapse or non-adherence to treatment. However, annotating for topic by hand is a time-consuming and subjective process (topics must first be agreed on by researchers, and annotators subsequently trained on this annotation scheme); we therefore examine the use of automatic topic modelling.

1.3 Topic modelling

Probabilistic topic modelling using Latent Dirichlet Allocation (LDA; Blei et al., 2003) has been previously used to extract topics from large corpora of texts, e.g. web documents and scientific articles. A "topic" consists of a cluster of words that frequently occur together. Using contextual clues, topic models can connect words with similar meanings and distinguish between uses of words with multiple meanings (see e.g. Steyvers and Griffiths, 2007). LDA uses unsupervised learning methods, and learns the topic distributions from the data itself, by iteratively adjusting priors (see Blei, 2012, for an outline of the algorithms used in LDA). Such techniques have been applied to structured dialogue, such as meetings (Purver et al., 2006) and tutoring dialogues (Arguello and Rosé, 2006) with encouraging results.

In the clinical domain, probabilistic topic modelling has been applied to patients' notes to discover relevant clinical concepts and connections between patients (Arnold et al., 2010). In terms of clinical *dialogue*, there are few studies which apply unsupervised methods to learning topic models, though recently this has become an active field of exploration. Angus et al. (2012) apply unsupervised methods to primary care clinical dialogues, to visualise shared content in communication in this domain. However, their data relies on only six dialogues, with the three training dialogues being produced in a role play situation. It is unclear whether using constructed dialogues as the baseline measure maps reliably to genuine dialogues. Additonally, though they did find differences in the patterns of communication based on how the patient had rated the encounter, their task was a descriptive one, not a predictive one and it is unclear if or how their methodology would scale up, especially given that they selected their testing dialogues on the basis of the patient evaluations.

Cretchley et al. (2010) applied unsupervised techniques to dialogues between patients with schizophrenia and their carers (either professional carers or family members). Patients and carers were instructed to talk informally and given a list of general interest topics such as sport and entertainment. They split their sample into two pre-defined communication styles ("low- or high- activity communicators") and described differences in the most common words spoken by each type depending on both the type of carer and the type of communicator. Once again, however, this was a descriptive exercise, on a very small number of dyads, and in choosing to predefine the participants by the amount of communicative activity they undertook they may have missed ways to differentiate between groups of patients that can be extracted from the data, rather than being pre-theoretic.

1.4 Research questions

The preliminary studies outlined above demonstrate some of the issues arising from using unsupervised topic modelling techniques to look at clinical dialogues. One of the main issues is in the interpretation of results. Studies described above used visualisations of the data to find patterns; one question that therefore arises is whether we can usefully interpret "topics" without these – for example, just by examining the most common words in a topic. Another question concerns the limited evidence that different styles of communication can be demonstrated using unsupervised topic modelling, and that these differences have a bearing on, for example, the patient's evaluations of the communication or their symptoms. Our main questions here are therefore:

- Does identification of topic allow prediction of symptoms and/or therapy outcomes?
- If so, can automatic topic modelling be used instead of manual annotation?
- Does automatic modelling produce topics that are interpretable and/or comparable to human judgements?

2 Data

This study used data from a larger study investigating clinical encounters in psychosis (McCabe et al., tion), collected between March 2006 and January 2008. 31 psychiatrists agreed to participate. Patients meeting Diagnostic and Statistical Manual-IV (APA) criteria for a diagnosis of schizophrenia or schizoaffective disorder attending psychiatric outpatient and assertive outreach clinics in three centres (one urban, one semi-urban and one rural) were asked to participate in the study. After complete description of the study to the subjects, written informed consent was obtained from 138 (40%) of those approached. Psychiatrist-patient consultations were then audio-visually recorded using digital video. The dialogues were transcribed, and these transcriptions, consisting only of the words spoken, form our dataset here. The consultations ranged in length, with the shortest consisting of only 617 words (lasting approximately 5 minutes), and the longest 13816 (lasting nearly an hour). The mean length of consultation was 3751 words.

2.1 Outcomes

Patients were interviewed at baseline, immediately after the consultation, by researchers not involved in the patients' care, to assess their symptoms. Both patients and psychiatrists filled in questionnaires evaluating their experience of the consultation at baseline, and psychiatrists were asked to assess each patient's adherence to treatment in a follow-up interview six months after the consultation. The measures obtained are described in more detail below.

2.1.1 Symptoms

Independent researchers assessed patients' symptoms at baseline on the 30-item Positive and Negative Syndrome Scale (PANSS, Kay et al., 1987). The scale assesses positive, negative and general symptoms and is rated on a scale of 1-7 (with higher scores indicating more severe symptoms). Positive symptoms represent a change in the patients' behaviour or thoughts and include sensory hallucinations and delusional beliefs. Negative symptoms represent a withdrawal or reduction in functioning, including blunted affect, and emotional withdrawal and alogia (poverty of speech). Positive and negative subscale scores ranged from 7 (absent) - 49 (extreme), general symptoms (such as anxiety) scores ranged from 16 (absent) - 112 (extreme). Inter-rater reliability using videotaped interviews for PANSS was good (Cohen's kappa=0.75).

2.1.2 Patient satisfaction

Patient satisfaction with the communication was assessed using the Patient Experience Questionnaire (PEQ, Steine et al., 2001). Three of the five subscales (12 questions) were used as the others were not relevant, having been developed for primary care. The three subscales were *communication experiences*, *communication barriers* and *emotions immediately after the visit*. For the communication subscales, items were measured on a 5-point Likert scale, with 1=disagree completely and 5=agree completely. The four items for the emotion scale were measured on a 7-point visual analogue scale, with opposing emotions at either end. A higher score indicates a better experience.

2.1.3 Therapeutic relationship

The Helping Alliance Scale (HAS, Priebe and Gruyters, 1993) was used after the consultation to assess both patients' and doctors' experience of the therapeutic relationship. The HAS has 5 items in the clinician version and 6 items in the patient version, with questions rated on a scale of 1-10. Items cover aspects of interpersonal relationships between patients and clinician and aspects of their judgment as to the degree of common understanding and the capability to provide or receive the necessary help, respectively. The scores from the individual items were averaged to provide a single value, with lower scores indicating a worse therapeutic relationship.

2.1.4 Adherence to treatment

Adherence to treatment was rated by the clinicians as good (>75%), average (25-75%) or poor (<25%) six months after the consultation. Due to the low incidence of poor ratings (only 8 dialogues), this was converted to a binary score of 1 for good adherence (89 patients), and 0 otherwise (37). Ratings were not available for the remaining 12 dialogues.

2.2 Hand-coded topics

Hermann et al. (in prep) annotated all 138 consultations for topics. First, an initial list of categories was developed by watching a subset of the consultations. The dialogues were then manually segmented and topics assigned to each segment, with the list of topic categories amended iteratively to ensure best fit and coverage of all relevant topics. A subset of 12 consultations was coded independently by two annotators, such that every utterance (and hence every word) was assigned to a single topic; inter-rater reliability was found to be good using Cohen's kappa ($\kappa = 0.71$). The final list of topics used, with descriptions, is outlined in Table 1.

Topic	Name	Description
01	Medication	Any discussion of medication, excluding side effects
02	Medication side effects	Side effects of medication
03	Daily activities	Includes activities such as education, employment, household chores, daily structure etc
04	Living situation	The life situation of the patient, including housing, finances, benefits, plans with life etc
05	Psychotic symptoms	Discussion on symptoms of psychosis such as hallucinations and delusional beliefs
06	Physical health	Any discussion on general physical health, physical illnesses, operations, etc
07	Non-psychotic symptoms	Discussion of mood symptoms, anxiety, obsessions, compulsions, phobias etc
08	Suicide and self harm	Intent, attempts or thoughts of self harm or suicide (past and present)
09	Alcohol, drugs & smoking	Current or past use of alcohol, drugs or cigarettes and their harmful effects
10	Past illness	Discussion of past history of psychiatric illnesses, including previous admissions and relapses
11	Mental health services	Care coordinator, community psychiatric nurse, social worker or home treatment team etc
12	Other services	Primary care services, social services, DVLA, employment agencies, police, housing etc
13	General chat	Includes introductions; general topics; weather; holidays; end of appointment courtesies
14	Explanation about illness	Patients diagnosis, including doctor explanations and patients questions about their illness
15	Coping strategies	Discussions around coping strategies that the patient is using or the doctor is advising
16	Relapse indicators	Relapse indicators and relapse prevention, including early warning signs
17	Treatment	General and psychological treatments, advice on managing anxiety, building confidence etc
18	Healthy lifestyle	Any advice on healthy lifestyle such as dietary advice, exercise, sleep hygiene etc
19	Relationships	Family members, friends, girlfriends, neighbours, colleagues and relationships etc
20	Other	Anything else. Includes e.g. humour, positive comments and non-specific complaints

Table 1: Hand-coded topic names and descriptions

3 Topic Modelling

The transcripts from the same 138 consultations were analysed using an unsupervised probabilistic topic model. The model was generated using the MAchine Learning for LanguagE Toolkit (MALLET, McCallum, 2002), using standard Latent Dirichlet Allocation (Blei et al., 2003) with the notion of *document* corresponding to the transcribed sequence of words spoken (by any speaker) in one consultation. As is conventional (see e.g. Salton and McGill, 1986), stop words (common words which do not contribute to the content of the talk, such as 'the' and 'to') were removed. The number of topics was specified as 20 to match the number of topics used by the human annotators (see above),[1] and the default setting of 1000 Gibbs sampling iterations was used. As an uneven distribution of topics was observed in the hand-coded topic data (see below), automatic hyperparameter optimisation was enabled to allow the prominence of topics and the skewedness of their associated word distributions to vary to best fit the data.

3.1 Interpretation

The resulting topics (probability distributions over words) were then assessed by experts for their interpretability in the context of consultations between psychiatrists and out-patients with schizophrenia. The top 20 most probable words in each topic were presented to two groups independently — one group of experts in the area of psychiatric research (of whom some members were also involved

[1]This is, of course, an arbitrary decision, and future work should investigate different numbers of topics.

in developing the hand-coded topics), and one group of experts in the area of communication and dialogue (without specific expertise in the context of psychiatry) — and each group produced text descriptions of the topics they felt they corresponded to. The two groups' interpretations strongly agreed in 13 of the 20 topic assignments (65%) and partially agreed (i.e. there was some overlap in the interpretations) in a further 3 topic assignments (i.e. in total, 80%).

Having assigned a tentative interpretation to the top word lists for each topic, the two groups reconvened to examine the occurrences of the topics in the raw transcripts, in order to validate these interpretations within the context of the discussion. Excerpts from the dialogues were chosen on the basis of the proportion of words assigned to each topic in the final iteration of the LDA sampling algorithm. Four excerpts were examined for each of the 20 topics, and a final interpretation for each was agreed.

The ease of giving the topic lists of most common words a coherent "interpretation" varied greatly. Some topics were easily given compact descriptions, for example topics 6, 12 and 18, whilst other word lists appeared more disparate. The list of topics and interpretations can be seen in Table 2.

	Interpretation	Example words from top 20
0	Sectioning/crisis	hospital, police, locked
1	Physical health - side-effects of medication and other medical issues	gp, injection, operation
2	Non-medical services - liaising with other services	letter, dla, housing
3	Ranting - negative descriptions of lifestyle etc	bloody, cope, mental
4	Meaningful activities - social functioning beyond the illness setting (e.g. work, study)	progress, work, friends
5	Making sense of psychosis	god, talking, reason
6	Sleep patterns	sleep, bed, night
7	Social stressors - other people who are stressors or helpful under stress	home, thought, told
8	Physical symptoms - e.g. pain, hyperventilating	breathing, breathe, burning
9	Physical tests - Anxiety/stress arising from physical tests	blood, tests, stress
10	Psychotic symptoms - e.g. voices, etc.	voices, hearing, evil
11	Reasurrance/positive feedback - also possibly progress	sort, work, sense
12	Substance use - alcohol/drugs	drinking, alcohol, cannabis
13	Family/lifestyle	mum, brother, shopping
14	Non-psychotic symptoms - incl. mood, paranoia, negative feelings	feel, mood, depression
15	Medication issues	medication, drugs, reduce
16	External support - positive social support (e.g. work, family, people)	good, people, happy
17	Weight management - weight issues in the context of drug side-effects	weight, diet, exercise
18	Medication regimen - dose, timings etc	milligrams, tablets, dose
19	Leisure - social relationships/social life etc	mates, pub, birthday

Table 2: Interpretations of LDA topics

3.2 Distribution

Figure 1 shows the distribution of the different topics across the whole corpus; for the automatic LDA version, this is determined from the most likely assignment of observed words to topics. The distribution is highly skewed, with the largest topic (16) accounting for about a fifth of all the data, and the smallest topic (3) only 1.4%. Once stop words had been removed the corpus consisted of 78,723 tokens. Nearly 18,000 of these (17,957) were therefore most likely to be assigned to topic 16, with just over 1000 (1063) in the smallest topic.

As can be seen from Figure 1, the distribution of automatic topics is consistent with the distribution from the hand-coded topics (Kolmogorov-Smirnov $D = 0.300, p = 0.275$). However, it is not clear that the topics themselves correspond so well. For the hand-coded topics, the topic with the highest probability is *medication*, followed by *general chat* and then *psychotic symptoms*; for the LDA topics, the most likely is *external support*, followed by *medication regimen* and *social stressors* – with *psychotic symptoms* only appearing much further down the list.

3.3 Cross-correlations between hand-coded and automatic topics

We next examined the correspondence between automatic and hand-coded topics directly. Of course, because of the differences in methods, we do not expect these to be equivalent; but examining similarities and differences helps validate (or otherwise) the interpretations given to the LDA topics, and determine whether the topics in fact pick out different aspects of the dialogues in each case.

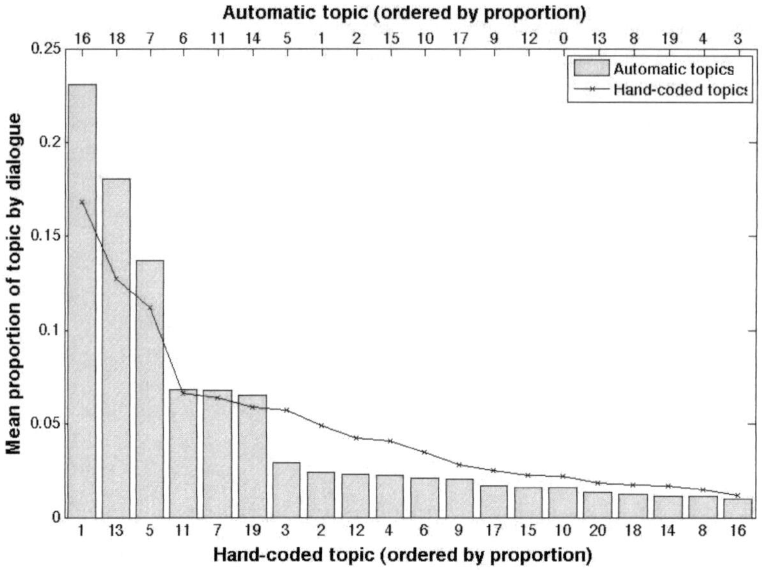

Figure 1: Distribution of topics

Table 3 shows correlations with coefficients greater than 0.3.[2] These correlations are calculated on the basis of the proportions of each topic in each dialogue; as such, these are overview figures across dialogues and do not tell us about topic assignment at a finer-grained level (for example, we know that highly correlated topics occur in the same dialogues, but not whether they occur in the same sequential sections of those dialogues).

Hand-coded topic	Automatic topic	r	p
Medication	Medication regimen	0.643	<0.001
Psychotic symptoms	Making sense of psychosis	0.357	<0.001
Psychotic symptoms	Psychotic symptoms	0.503	<0.001
Physical health	Physical health	0.603	<0.001
Non-psychotic symptoms	Sleep patterns	0.376	<0.001
Suicide and self-harm	Weight management	0.386	<0.001
Alcohol, drugs and smoking	Substance use	0.651	<0.001
Mental health services	Non-medical services	0.396	<0.001
General chat	Sectioning/crisis	0.364	<0.001
Treatment	Medication issues	0.394	<0.001
Healthy lifestyle	Weight management	0.517	<0.001
Relationships	Ranting	0.391	<0.001
Relationships	Social stressors	0.418	<0.001
Relationships	Leisure	0.341	<0.001

Table 3: Correlations between hand-coded and automatic topic distributions

From the data above we can see that some of the topics match up well, suggesting that in certain cases the LDA topic model is picking out similar aspects of the content. Examples are the high correlations between the hand and automatically coded *substance misuse* and *physical health* topics. Given the relative prominence of the two topics, the high correlation between *medication* and *medication regimen* suggests that the LDA topic model is picking out a subset of the talk on medication. This could be linked to the fact that though there may be many different ways of talking about medication (potentially depending on the type of drug, the patient's history etc) that are understandable to human annotators, there is a smaller set of talk about medication which refers to e.g. dosages which is being discovered by LDA topic modelling. Similar considerations may be at play with the link between *healthy lifestyle* and *weight management*, and *non-psychotic symptoms* and *sleep issues*.

More interestingly the hand-coded *psychotic symptoms* topic is highly correlated with two automatic topics about psychotic symptoms. Looking at the contexts of these topics, it appears that there

[2]Note that this is an arbitrary cut-off point; other smaller significant correlations also exist in the data.

may be differences in the ways people talk about their psychotic symptoms depending on whether they are describing the symptoms per se, or looking to make sense of their psychotic symptoms in a wider context.

Interesting differences in the two codings can also be seen in the correlations with *relationships*, which could illustrate different ways is which they are discussed, both negative (*ranting*), and positive (*leisure*). This suggests that the LDA topics are picking up additional factors of the communication in addition to the content.

4 Prediction of Target Variables

We now turn to examining the association between topics and the target variables we would like to predict: symptoms, doctor and patient evaluations of the therapy, and patient outcomes (specifically, adherence to treatment).

4.1 Correlations with symptoms

Patterns of symptoms are known to affect communication, and we therefore assessed whether there were correlations between what was talked about, as indexed by hand coded or automatically coded topic, and the three PANSS symptom scales (positive, negative, general).

	Symptom scale	Topic	r	p
Hand-coded	positive	daily activities	-0.249	0.004
		psychotic symptoms	0.487	<0.001
	negative	daily activities	-0.211	0.015
		psychotic symptoms	0.206	0.018
	general	daily activities	-0.254	0.003
		psychotic symptoms	0.383	<0.001
		healthy lifestyle	-0.235	0.007
		suicide and self harm	0.230	0.008
Automatic	positive	ranting	0.265	0.002
		making sense of psychosis	0.378	<0.001
		physical tests	0.233	0.007
		psychotic symptoms	0.316	<0.001
	negative	weight management	-0.202	0.019
	general	ranting	0.234	0.007
		making sense of psychosis	0.316	<0.001

Table 4: Correlations between symptoms and topics

As can be seen from Table 4[3], for the hand coded topics, all three symptom scales were negatively correlated with *daily activities* (consultations with more ill patients contained less talk about *daily activities*) and positively correlated with talk about *psychotic symptoms*. Higher general symptoms were also associated with less talk about *healthy lifestyle*, and more about *suicide and self-harm*.

For the automatically extracted topics, consultations with patients with more positive symptoms had more talk in the categories of *ranting*, *making sense of psychosis*, *physical tests* and *psychotic symptoms*. Consultations with patients with worse negative symptoms had less talk about *weight management*. As with the hand-coded topics there was some overlap between positive and general symptoms, with general symptoms positively correlated with *ranting* and *making sense of psychosis*. These correlations also served as a validation measure of some of the topics, and their interpretations.

4.2 Classification experiments

We performed a series of classification experiments, to investigate whether the probability distributions of topics could enable automatic detection of patient and doctor evaluations of the consultation, symptoms and adherence. In each case, we used the Weka machine learning toolkit (Hall et al., 2009) to pre-process data, and a decision tree classifier (J48) and the support vector machine implementation Weka LibSVM (EL-Manzalawy and Honavar, 2005) as classifiers. Variables to be predicted were binarised into groups of equal size prior to analysis, and for the adherence measure a balanced

[3]Table 4 shows correlations above 0.2 only.

	Topics and Dr/P factors		Topics and P factors		Topics only		Dr/P factors only	
Measure	J48	SVM	J48	SVM	J48	SVM	J48	SVM
HAS Dr	**75.8**	**71.2**	47.0	56.8	50.8	56.8	**72.0**	**71.2**
HAS P	46.3	49.3	59.0	53.7	50.7	47.0	51.5	52.2
PANSS pos	58.0	59.5	58.8	49.6	**61.1**	58.0	45.8	59.5
PANSS neg	58.3	59.1	57.6	**62.1**	**61.4**	57.6	54.5	52.3
PANSS gen	51.9	55.0	55.0	57.3	55.7	59.5	51.9	53.4
PEQ comm	50.0	56.0	53.7	59.7	55.2	55.2	57.5	**61.2**
PEQ comm barr	50.7	**61.9**	56.0	50.7	52.2	52.2	49.3	**60.4**
PEQ emo	51.2	45.7	47.2	48.0	51.2	49.6	57.5	50.0
Adherence (balanced)	51.4	**66.2**	47.3	50.0	51.4	44.6	47.3	56.8

Table 5: Accuracy of hand-coded topics with different feature groups

	Topics and Dr/P factors		Topics and P factors		Topics only	
Measure	J48	SVM	J48	SVM	J48	SVM
HAS Dr	**75.0**	**75.0**	**62.9**	50.8	**65.2**	**62.9**
HAS P	49.3	48.5	50.7	50.7	53.7	47.0
PANSS pos	45.0	58.8	47.3	44.3	51.1	50.4
PANSS neg	50.8	52.3	56.1	56.1	48.5	50.8
PANSS gen	47.3	50.4	52.7	48.9	53.4	48.9
PEQ comm	51.5	56.0	54.5	50.7	56.7	53.7
PEQ comm barr	56.7	**60.4**	53.7	47.8	51.5	56.0
PEQ emo	57.5	49.6	48.8	51.2	52.8	53.5
Adherence (balanced)	47.3	54.1	47.3	44.6	47.3	51.4

Table 6: Accuracy of automatically extracted topics with different feature groups

subset of 74 cases was used. All experiments used 5-fold cross-validation, and the experiments using an SVM classifier used a radial bias function with the best values for cost and gamma determined by a grid search in each case.

Tables 5 and 6 show the accuracy figures for each predicted variable, using a variety of different feature subsets. Doctor factors are the gender and identity of the doctor. Patient factors are the gender and age of the patient, and also the total number of words spoken by both patient and doctor. Topic factors are the total number of words in that topic for the hand-coded topics; and an equivalent value for the automatic topics calculated by multiplying the topic's posterior probability for a dialogue by the total number of words.

From Tables 5 and 6[4] we can see that there are different patterns of results for the different measures. For the therapeutic relationship (HAS) measures, including doctor factors gives an accuracy of over 70% in all cases, with the identity of the psychiatrist the most important factor in the decision trees. However, although allowing us a reasonably good fit to the data, the inclusion of the doctor's identity as a feature means that this is not a generalisable result; we would not be able to utilise the information from this factor in predicting the HAS score of a consultation with a new doctor. In this respect, the 65% accuracy when using only the 20 coarse-grained automatic topics is encouraging. In the decision tree, the highest node is *social stressors*, with a high amount of talk in this category indicating a low rating of the therapeutic relationship from the doctor (66 low/21 high). If there was less talk about *social stressors*, the next highest node is *sleep patterns*, with more talk in this area indicating a greater likelihood of a good therapeutic relationship rating (29 high/3 low). Next, more talk about *non-psychotic symptoms* leads to low ratings (11 low/3 high), and more *reassurance*, leads to a better therapeutic relationship. Interestingly, automatic topics give better accuracy than manual topics when used alone.

For adherence, the best accuracy is achieved by a model which includes doctor features as well as hand-coded topics. Good physician communication is known to increase adherence (Zolnierek and DiMatteo, 2009) and in this sample, adherence was also related to the doctor's evaluation of the

[4] Accuracy values of over 60% are shown in bold.

therapeutic relationship, with 29 of the 37 non-adherent patients rated as having a poor therapeutic relationship by the doctor ($\chi 2 = 13.364, p < 0.001$).

Given this, it is surprising that we can predict the therapeutic relationship reasonably well using only automatic topics, but not adherence. Topics also do not appear to give useful performance when predicting patient ratings of the therapeutic relationship (HAS P), or patient evaluations of the consultation (PEQ), although doctor/patient factors seem to have some predictive power. Note that low-level lexical features have shown success in predicting both adherence and patient ratings (Howes et al., 2012a, achieved f-scores of around 70%).

The best predictors for the different types of symptoms are also low, but here the hand-coded topics do better than the automatic topics, with accuracies of 61% for both positive and negative symptoms. For positive symptoms, perhaps unsurprisingly, the decision tree only has one node; if there is more talk on the topic of *psychotic symptoms*, then the patient is likely to have higher positive symptoms (or vice versa). However, in this respect, especially given the cross-correlations discussed above, it is surprising that the automatic topics do not allow any prediction of symptoms at above chance levels. For negative symptoms, patients are likely to have more negative symptoms in consultations with little talk on either *healthy lifestyle* or *daily activities*.

5 Discussion

While both LDA and hand-coded topics seem to have some predictive power, they have different effects for different target variables. Automatic topics do not allow prediction of symptoms, where manual topics do – even though there is a correlation between their corresponding topics relating to psychotic symptoms. This may suggest that LDA used in this way is discovering topics which are a subset of the manual topics: discussion of symptoms may be wider and include more different conversational phenomena than suggested purely by symptom-related lexical items. On the other hand, LDA topics appear to be better at predicting evaluations of the therapeutic relationship; here, one possible explanation may be that LDA is producing "topics" which capture aspects of style or structure rather than purely content. Further investigation might reveal whether examination of the relevant LDA topics can reveal important aspects of communication style – particularly that of the doctor, given that doctor identity factors also improve prediction of this measure, and are related to patients subsequent adherence.

Although the results from this exploratory study are limited, they are encouraging. We have used only very coarse-grained notions of topics, and a simplistic document-style LDA model, so there is much potential for further research. Using a more dialogue-related model that takes account of topic sequential structure (e.g. Purver et al., 2006) or one that can incorporate stylistic material separately to content, as done for function vs content words by Griffiths and Steyvers (2004) should allow us to produce models that better describe the data and can be used to discover more directly what aspects of the communication between doctors and patients with schizophrenia are associated with their symptoms, therapeutic relationship and adherence behaviour.

References

Angus, D., B. Watson, A. Smith, C. Gallois, and J. Wiles (2012). Visualising conversation structure across time: Insights into effective doctor-patient consultations. *PLoS ONE 7*(6), 1–12.

Arguello, J. and C. Rosé (2006). Topic segmentation of dialogue. In *Proceedings of the HLT-NAACL Workshop on Analyzing Conversations in Text and Speech*, New York, NY.

Arnold, C., S. El-Saden, A. Bui, and R. Taira (2010). Clinical case-based retrieval using latent topic analysis. In *AMIA Annual Symposium Proceedings*, Volume 2010, pp. 26. American Medical Informatics Association.

Blei, D. (2012). Probabilistic topic models. *Communications of the ACM 55*(4), 77–84.

Blei, D., A. Ng, and M. Jordan (2003). Latent Dirichlet allocation. *Journal of Machine Learning Research 3*, 993–1022.

Cretchley, J., C. Gallois, H. Chenery, and A. Smith (2010). Conversations between carers and people with schizophrenia: a qualitative analysis using leximancer. *Qualitative Health Research 20*(12), 1611–1628.

EL-Manzalawy, Y. and V. Honavar (2005). *WLSVM: Integrating LibSVM into Weka Environment.* Software available at `http://www.cs.iastate.edu/~yasser/wlsvm`.

Fenton, W., C. Blyler, and R. Heinssen (1997). Determinants of medication compliance in schizophrenia: Empirical and clinical findings. *Schizophrenia Bulletin 23*(4), 637.

Griffiths, T. and M. Steyvers (2004). Finding scientific topics. *Proceedings of the National Academy of Science 101*, 5228–5235.

Hall, M., E. Frank, G. Holmes, B. Pfahringer, P. Reutemann, and I. H. Witten (2009). The WEKA data mining software: An update. *SIGDKDD Explorations 11*(1), 10–18.

Hermann, P., M. Lavelle, S. Mehnaz, and R. McCabe (in preparation). What do psychiatrists and patients with schizophrenia talk about in psychiatric encounters?

Howes, C., M. Purver, R. McCabe, P. G. T. Healey, and M. Lavelle (2012a). Helping the medicine go down: Repair and adherence in patient-clinician dialogues. In *Proceedings of the 16th Workshop on the Semantics and Pragmatics of Dialogue (SemDial 2012)*, Paris.

Howes, C., M. Purver, R. McCabe, P. G. T. Healey, and M. Lavelle (2012b). Predicting adherence to treatment for schizophrenia from dialogue transcripts. In *Proceedings of the 13th Annual Meeting of the Special Interest Group on Discourse and Dialogue (SIGDIAL 2012 Conference)*, Seoul, South Korea, pp. 79–83. Association for Computational Linguistics.

Kay, S., A. Fiszbein, and L. Opfer (1987). The positive and negative syndrome scale (PANSS) for schizophrenia. *Schizophrenia bulletin 13*(2), 261.

McCabe, R., C. Heath, T. Burns, S. Priebe, and J. Skelton (2002). Engagement of patients with psychosis in the consultation: conversation analytic study. *British Medical Journal 325*(7373), 1148–1151.

McCabe, R., M. Lavelle, S. Bremner, D. Dodwell, P. G. T. Healey, R. Laugharne, S. Priebe, and A. Snell (in preparation). Shared understanding in psychiatrist-patient communication: Association with treatment adherence in schizophrenia.

McCallum, A. K. (2002). MALLET: A machine learning for language toolkit. http://mallet.cs.umass.edu.

Ong, L., J. De Haes, A. Hoos, and F. Lammes (1995). Doctor-patient communication: a review of the literature. *Social science & medicine 40*(7), 903–918.

Priebe, S. and T. Gruyters (1993). The role of the helping alliance in psychiatric community care: A prospective study. *Journal of Nervous and Mental Disease 181*(9), 552–557.

Purver, M., K. Körding, T. Griffiths, and J. Tenenbaum (2006). Unsupervised topic modelling for multi-party spoken discourse. In *Proceedings of the 21st International Conference on Computational Linguistics and 44th Annual Meeting of the Association for Computational Linguistics (COLING-ACL)*, Sydney, Australia, pp. 17–24. Association for Computational Linguistics.

Salton, G. and M. McGill (1986). *Introduction to modern information retrieval.* McGraw-Hill, Inc.

Steine, S., A. Finset, and E. Laerum (2001). A new, brief questionnaire (PEQ) developed in primary health care for measuring patients' experience of interaction, emotion and consultation outcome. *Family practice 18*(4), 410–418.

Steyvers, M. and T. Griffiths (2007). Probabilistic topic models. *Handbook of latent semantic analysis 427*(7), 424–440.

Zolnierek, K. and M. DiMatteo (2009). Physician communication and patient adherence to treatment: a meta-analysis. *Medical care 47*(8), 826.

Figurative Language in Swedish Clinical Texts

Dimitrios Kokkinakis
Centre for Language Technology and the Swedish Language Bank,
University of Gothenburg, Sweden
dimitrios.kokkinakis@svenska.gu.se

Abstract

Automated processing of clinical texts is commonly faced with various less exposed, and not so regularly discussed linguistically complex problems that need to be addressed. One of these issues concerns the usage of figurative language. Figurative language implies the use of words that go beyond their ordinary meaning, a linguistically complex and challenging problem and also a problem that causes great difficulty for the field of natural language processing (NLP). The problem is equally prevalent in both general language and also in various sublanguages, such as clinical medicine. Therefore we believe that a comprehensive model of e.g. clinical language processing needs to account for figurative language usage, and this paper provides a description, and preliminary results towards this goal. Since the empirical, clinical data used in the study is limited in size, there is no formal distinction made between different sub-classifications of figurative language. e.g., metaphors, idioms or simile. We illustrate several types of figurative expressions in the clinical discourse and apply a rather quantitative and corpus-based level analysis. The main research questions that this paper asks are whether there are traces of figurative language (or at least a subset of such types) in patient-doctor and patient-nurse interactions, how can they be found in a convenient way and whether these are transferred in the electronic health records and to what degree.

1 Introduction

Automated processing of clinical texts with the intention to link all important text fragments to various established terminologies and ontologies for relation or event extraction is commonly faced with various less exposed, and not so regularly discussed linguistically motivated issues that needs to be addressed. One of these issues is the usage of figurative language. Figurative language, that is the use of words that go beyond their ordinary meaning, is not only a linguistically complex and challenging problem but also a problem that causes great difficulty for the field of natural language processing (NLP), both for the processing of general language and of various sublanguages, such as clinical medicine. Therefore we believe that a comprehensive model of e.g. clinical language processing needs to account for figurative language usage, and this paper provides a description, and preliminary results towards this goal. Since the empirical, clinical data used in the study is limited in size, there is no formal distinction made between different sub-classifications of figurative language. e.g., metaphors, idioms or simile. As a matter of fact, all these types of expressions form a continuum with fuzzy boundaries [9], and most of the NLP-oriented approaches discussed in the past have used either very large data for the analysis or hand annotates samples [17], a situation that has been prohibitive so far in our project. Therefore distinction is solely based on a more general level, namely between literal versus figurative language, and on a more quantitative and corpus-based level, supported with concrete examples that illustrate several types of figurative expressions in the clinical discourse. The main research questions that this paper asks are whether there are traces of figurative language (or at least a subset of such types) in patient-doctor and patient-nurse interactions, how can they be found in a convenient way and whether these are transferred in the electronic health records and to what degree.

2 Theoretical Background (Idioms, Metaphors and Similes)

Figurative language has been in a focus among several scholars during a very long period. Cognitive linguists, for instance ([12], [11]), have been studying figurative language for many years under the assumption that word meaning is not "fixed" but is rather a function of perspective, therefore compositionality (the degree to which the features of the parts of a multi word expression combine to predict the features of the whole) can only be achieved if context is taken into consideration. Figurative language, compared to literal language, refers to simple words, and most frequently, to multiword expressions that deviate from their defined meaning by e.g., exaggerating or altering the usual meanings of the constituent words [18]. Figurative language, and its realization into various rhetorical devices, i.e. figures of speech, departs from literal meaning to achieve some form of a particular effect on the listener or reader.

There are several different, but related, types of such figures of speech but here we mainly investigate just three of the most common ones, namely idioms, metaphors and similes using a combination of simple and flexible automated techniques. An *idiom* (e.g., "He is pulling my leg") is an expression consisting of a combination of words that have a figurative meaning. Idiomatic expressions are usually presumed to be figures of speech contradicting the principle of compositionality. Many idioms appear in language first as metaphors and if during some time period, a large part of a population finds them interesting, and/or useful, then they become a fixed part of the language as idioms. A *metaphor* (e.g., "All the world's a stage") is a literary figure of speech that describes a subject by asserting that it is, on some point of comparison, the same as another otherwise unrelated object. A metaphor asserts that one thing is another thing, not just that one is *like* another, such as in the case of *simile* (e.g., "He fights like a lion") which is a figure of speech that directly compares two different things. Similes usually employ the words "as" and "like" or other comparative words such as "than". A simile differs from a metaphor in that the latter compares two unlike things by saying that the one thing is the other thing. Similes can be negative, too, asserting that two things are unlike in one or more respects. Finally, previous work has shown that common figures of speech, such as idioms and metaphors, also involve some degree of lexical and syntactic variability, in the sense that, for instance, some allow pluralization while some not.

3 Previous Research

Some of the work that has been conducted from a strong corpus based and/or NLP perspective includes the work by [8] who focus on a particular class of English idiomatic expression, i.e., those that involve the combination of a verb plus a noun in its direct object position. Fazly & Stevenson [8] investigated a lexicon-based method were a lexical and syntactic flexibility (e.g., verbal inflection; pluralization; internal modification; use of determiner types; passivization) was allowed in a restrictive form. Among the idioms examined, some exhibited limited morphosyntactic flexibility, while others were more syntactically flexible. For instance, the idiom "shoot the breeze" can undergo verbal inflection, i.e. "shot the breeze", but not internal modification or passivization, i.e. "the breeze was shot" [4]. A main interpretative approach to non-literal use detection (e.g., metaphors) is the investigation of whether there are some sort of selectional preference violations in a given context; *cf.* [19] and [15]. According to Wilks, selectional restrictions are the semantic constraints that a verb places onto its arguments, "a car drinks gasoline", since the English verb "to drink" tends to have a human or animal as the subject and food or potable liquid as the direction object, respectively. In a similar path, Hank [10], in his example "political storm", discusses how adjectives can be classified in order to pick out an appropriate subset, by first distinguishing between adjectives that identify kinds of storms as natural phenomena and those where the word is used metaphorically. If the correct interpretation of e.g. "storm" is to be activated, it is necessary first to distinguish between adjectives that identify storms as natural phenomena and then those where the word is used in a non-literal sense. Other work is specifically geared towards metaphor recognition [14]. For instance, two kinds of metaphorical language is distinguished, "conventional metaphors", mostly idiomatic expressions, that become a part of an ordinary discourse, and "creative metaphors", which are distinctly novel or ad hoc uses of language, since neither the creator nor the audience has encountered the metaphor before. Creative metaphors are frequently used in conversation to describe an emotional experience [5]. Birke & Sarkar [2] presented a system for automatically classifying literal and non literal usages of phrasal and expression verbs, for example ”throw away”, through nearly unsupervised word-sense disambiguation and various clustering techniques based on models build on hand-annotated data. Finally, figurative usage seems to be an important research topic in the medical domain and there is some evidence that supports this claim. For example, it has been shown that figurative language has an active role in the narratives of patients with cancer. Such non-literal usage, e.g. metaphors, can bridge the gap between the cancer experience and the world of technology and treatment, helping patients to symbolically control their illness [13] while other studies have looked at how non-literal language shifts throughout a person's recovery period [3]. We believe that detection of figurative language can play an important role both for the deep understanding of the discourse and communication interplay, and particularly, also for the part of NLP that involves automatic text understanding, where figurative language is considered a serious bottleneck [16].

4 Experimental Setting

This study is part of an ongoing larger project which investigates how complex, vague and long-standing symptoms with no identified organic cause are put into context, interpreted and acted upon in primary health-care interactions. It is based on studying interactions between patients and nurses giving advice over telephone, consultations between patients and physicians, interviews and study patients' medical records and case notes. Eighteen eligible patients who have contacted their primary health care centre by telephone, have had at least eight physical consultations with nurses or physicians in the last 12 months and with a majority of the symptoms within this time span with no clear organic or psychiatric cause were selected for the project. At the end, and due to some practical considerations only data from 16 patients was finally used (75,000 tokens). The overall expected results is to facilitate the development of future interventions aimed at decreasing the morbidity due to Medically Unexplained Symptoms (MUS) and give further insights into the problem. There is no generally accepted diagnostic criteria for such Medically Unexplained Symptoms, but one proposed definition is ”one or more physical symptoms which have been present at least three months, cause the patient clinically significant distress or impairment and cannot be explained by any recognizable physical disease” [7]. Common symptoms among MUS patients are: *headaches, dizziness, fatigue, dyspepsia, bloatedness, myalgia, joint pain, facial pain, pelvic pains, lower back pain, cervical pain and slowness of thoughts.*

The chosen method is corpus based and is geared onto a rather quantitative analysis of the figurative language phenomenon in Swedish clinical texts. The approach we follow is basically a heuristic pattern matching approach which looks at lexically derived idiomatic keywords and their order in a sentence, with certain variation allowed. If a string fragment corresponding to a particular rule or pattern is found it is annotated. All sentences with annotations are then manually analyzed. The main instruments we make use of are large lists of available idiomatic expressions (idioms and metaphors) extracted from various monolingual lexical resources for written Swedish, roughly 6,000 idiomatic expressions as well as from several Internet sites, e.g., from `http://www.livet.se/ord/k%C3%A4lla/Idiom/`. We make also use of a list of string matching patterns, essentially rules, manually developed particularly for similes. The extracted list of idiomatic expressions is modeled as a finite state recognizer which permits a controlled form of lexical and syntactic variability. This variability is modeled as regular expressions with optional slot fillers that may or may not be filled by string fragments during processing. For instance, for the Swedish idiom: *tappa sugen* (lit. ”drop the craving”, i.e., ”give up”, ”lose interest”) we allow both inflection for the verb *tappa* (e.g., *tappade*, i.e., ”lost”) and also the possibility of intervening other words, usually one to three arbitrary words (e.g., *tappa inte sugen*, i.e. ”not give up”; *tappa hon inte sugen*, i.e. ”she did not give up”). For similes we use a limited list of characteristic single words or very short combinations of words, and their part of speech, in these rules, for instance *är som en/ett*, i.e. ”is like a”; *som en/ett*, i.e. ”like a” and *likt* or *liksom*, i.e. ”like”. These are modeled in a similar manner as before, by using regular expression patterns. Such a pattern (in a simplified form) may look like the following way: *Determiner? Adjective* (Pronoun/Noun) (är/other verbs) som (en/ett) Adjective* Noun* (where the symbol "/" is meant here to function as a disjunction). Here, however, we do not allow much variability since there is a significant risk of allowing the recognition of a large number of false positives and spurious results. However, we do allow gender variability *en* or *ett* and limited inflection.

5 Results

The results from the application of the previously outlined method were manual analyzed in order to get deeper insights into: a) the performance of the automatic recognition (predominantly from a *precision score* perspective) of the approach b) get an idea of the magnitude of the identified figurative expressions in the clinical data and c) get some guidance on whether figurative expressions are transferred from the patient-doctor and patient-nurse interactions into the electronic health records and to what degree. Finally, we would also like to find out which new figurative expressions are in the data and not captured by the existing resources; for instance are these *creative metaphors* or other types. However, due to time constraints this topic was not prioritized for the time being and thus not elaborated in detail.

Although the available data is limited in size there was a fairly large number of instances that could be identified, and some of those were rather creative, interesting and relevant for their context. In the electronic health records 143 (69 diferent) figurative, multiword expression could be identified (10 similes). Examples of both include: *ta sitt liv*, i.e. lit: "take your life", "commit suicide"; *kasta vatten*, i.e. lit. "to throw water", "to urinate" and *gå ner i vikt*, i.e. lit. "to go down in weight", "to lose weight"; and for similes *...ont som ett sug i magen* i.e. "...hurts like a suction in the stomach". In the transcribed interactions, which were much limited in size, 105 (42 diferent) figurative expression could be identified (21 similes). Examples of both include: *ett oskrivet blad*, i.e. lit. "an unwritten paper", "pure and innocent"; *det spelar ingen roll*, i.e. lit. "it does not play any role", "it does not matter"; and *hålla tummarna*, i.e. lit. "to hold the thumbs", "to wish for luck"; and for similes *diskbråck ... det är som en blixt*, i.e. "intervertebral disc displacement ... is like a flash from the sky".

From the manual analysis of all annotations (248), we could obtain an overall precision score of 72.1% (calculated as *Precision = true positives/true positives+false positives*; recall was not measured). The number of false positives (items incorrectly labeled) was 69 and the majority were falsely annotated similes triggered by the designed patterns, since due to their rather very general nature also identified a number of spurious candidates; for instance *...i Aquacel som en tamponad*, i.e. "...adds the Aquacel like/as a tamponade" or *...det är en rädsla*, i.e. "...it is a fear" (unclear pronominal reference). Finally, there was a 10.8% overlap between the annotation in the records and the transcribed dialogues.

6 Discussion and Future Work

There are several different types of figurative language in various discourse contexts with a high frequency of use, and in this paper we have investigated whether a subset of such expressions exist in Swedish clinical data. The preliminary results showed some very clear traces of such language and a large number could be identified using available lexical resources with high precision. However, recall is also important and future plans also include means to identify novel idiomatic expressions and/or other types of figurative language that seem to prevail in some of the clinical data. For instance, in the transcribed dialogues there is an overwhelming number of onomatopoetic expressions (i.e., imitation of a sound made by or associated with its referent, such as "wow" and "pff"). We would like to find out which new figurative expressions are in the data and not captured by the existing resources. Are these for instance *creative metaphors* or other types and of what kind. Through preliminary manual analysis we could identify several novel figurative expressions and predominantly in the transcribed dialogues, such as: *emotionell rutschelkana*, i.e. "emotional slide"; *går genom svarta hål*, i.e. "go through black holes"; *lärt känna nya sidor av dig själv*, i.e. "get to know new sides of yourself"; *sakta bygga från fötterna till huvud*, i.e. "slowly build from the feet to the head"; *bakom den människa/person*, i.e. "behind that person" and a smaller number in the records, e.g. *väldigt utbränd*, i.e. "very burned out". In such interactions, the ability to recognize and understand patients use of figurative language can provide clinicians with means of evaluating personality and styles of thinking.

As a future task it would be also highly relevant to qualitatively investigate the reasons why figurative language is present in the health records. Does it depend on lack of understanding from the coders side (usually a contact nurse); is it simply a convenient way to describe symptoms and states; is there lack of appropriate nomenclature? Moreover, an idiom type often has a literal interpretation as well. Therefore, the exploration of e.g. use of informative prior knowledge about the overall syntactic behavior of potentially-idiomatic expressions to determine whether an instance of the expression is used idiomatically or not, is of great importance for many (semantically oriented) NLP applications [6], an issue that requires more studies, particularly in critical domains where the distinction can have severe consequences. Moreover, the identification of figurative expressions, which describe physical or emotional symptoms, is a very useful supporting component, since these important expressions can be then automatically linked to existing medical ontologies and enhance e.g., decision support or other systems.

Currently, the experimentation is based on limited amount of data, therefore it is difficult to draw clear conclusions as to the magnitude of the impact the ability to identify idiomatic and figurative expressions would have on improving medical NLP or clinical care delivery. However, larger scale studies for other languages and domains have shown to be useful in many applications. Moreover, like sentiment analysis or opinion extraction, computational figurative identification can provide an understanding of the framings or conceptualizations used in various communities or subdomains [1].

References

[1] E. Baumer and B. Tomlinson. Computational metaphor identification in communities of blogs. *ICWSM. Proceedings of the Second International Conf. on Weblogs and Social Media. Seattle, USA, AAAI Press.*, 2008.

[2] J. Birke and A. Sarkar. A clustering approach for the nearly unsupervised recognition of non-literal language. *Proceedings of the 11th EACL. Trento, Italy.*, 30:329–336, 2006.

[3] C. Boylstein, M. Rittman, and R. Hinojosa. Metaphor shifts in stroke recovery. *Health Commun.*, 21(3):279–87, 2007.

[4] LJ. Brinton and E. Closs Traugott. Lexicalization and language change. *Cambridge University Press.*, page 55, 2005.

[5] R. Carter. *Language and creativity: The art of common talk.* Routledge, New York., 2004.

[6] P. Cook, A. Fazly, and S. Stevenson. Pulling their weight: Exploiting syntactic forms for the automatic identif ication of idiomatic expressions in context. *Proceedings of the ACL Workshop on A Broader Perspective on Multiword Expressions. Prague.*, pages 41–48, 2007.

[7] R. Peveler R. *et al.* Medically unexplained physical symptoms in primary care: a comparison of self-report screening questionnaires and clinical opinion. *J Psychosom Res.*, 42(3):245–252, 1997.

[8] P. A. Fazly and S. Stevenson. Automatically constructing a lexicon of verb phrase idiomatic combinations. *Proceedings of the 11th EACL. Trento, Italy.*, pages 337–344, 2006.

[9] RW. Gibbs. Literal meaning and psychological theory. *Cognitive Science*, 8:275–304, 1984.

[10] P. Hanks. The syntagmatics of metaphor and idiom. *International J of Lexicography*, 17:3, 2004.

[11] G. Lakoff and M. Johnson. *Metaphors We Live By.* University of Chicago Press, Chicago., 1980.

[12] R. W. Langacker. *Concept, Image, and Symbol. The Cognitive Basis of Grammar.* Berlin: Mouton de Gruyter., 1990.

[13] C. Laranjeira. The role of narrative and metaphor in the cancer life story: a theoretical analysis. *Med Health Care Philos.*, 2012.

[14] Group Pragglejaz. Mip: A method for identifying metaphorically used words in discourse metaphor and symbol. *Lawrence Erlbaum Associates, Inc*, 22(1):1–39, 2007.

[15] P. Resnik. Selectional constraints: an information-theoretic model and its computational realization. *Cognition*, 61:127–159, 1996.

[16] E. Shutova. Models of metaphor in nlp. *Proceedings of the 48th Annual Meeting of the Association for Computational Linguistics. Uppsala, Sweden.*, pages 688–697, 2010.

[17] E. Shutova and S. Teufel. Metaphor corpus annotated for source - target domain mappings. *Proceedings of the Conference on Language Resources and Evaluation (LREC). Malta.*, pages 3255–3261, 2010.

[18] L. Sikos, S. Windisch Brown, A. E. Kim1, L. A. Michaelis, and M. Palmer. Figurative language: 'meaning' is often more than just a sum of the parts. *Association for the Advancement of AI (AAAI). Conf. on Biologically Inspired Cognitive Architectures (BICA). Virginia, USA.*, 2008.

[19] Y. Wilks. Making preferences more active. *Artificial Intelligence. Reprinted in N. V. Findler, Associative Networks. New York: Academic Press.*, 11(3), 1978.

Evaluating the Use of Empirically Constructed Lexical Resources for Named Entity Recognition

Siddhartha Jonnalagadda[1], Trevor Cohen[2], Stephen Wu[1], Hongfang Liu[1], Graciela Gonzalez[3]

[1]Department of Health Sciences Research, Mayo Clinic, Rochester, MN, USA

[2]School of Biomedical Informatics, University of Texas Health Science Center, Houston, TX, USA

[3]Department of Biomedical Informatics, Arizona State University, Phoenix, AZ, USA

Abstract – Because of privacy concerns and the expense involved in creating an annotated corpus, the existing small annotated corpora might not have sufficient number of examples for statistically learning to extract all the named-entities precisely. In this work, we evaluate what value may lie in automatically generated features based on distributional semantics when using machine-learning named entity recognition (NER). The features we generated and experimented with include n-nearest words, support vector machine (SVM)-regions, and term clustering, all of which are considered semantic (or distributional semantic) features. The addition of n-nearest words feature resulted in a greater increase in F-score than adding a manually constructed lexicon to a baseline system that extracts medical concepts from clinical notes. Although the need for relatively small annotated corpora for retraining is not obviated, lexicons empirically derived from unannotated text can not only supplement manually created lexicons, but replace them. This phenomenon is observed in extracting concepts both from biomedical literature and clinical notes.

Background

One of the most time-consuming tasks faced by a Natural Language Processing (NLP) researcher or practitioner trying to adapt a machine-learning–based NER system to a different domain is the creation, compilation, and customization of the needed lexicons. Lexical resources, such as lexicons of concept classes are considered necessary to improve the performance of NER. It is typical for medical informatics researchers to implement modularized systems that cannot be generalized (Stanfill et al. 2010). As the work of constructing or customizing lexical resources needed for these highly specific systems is human-intensive, automatic generation is a desirable alternative. It might be possible that empirically created lexical resources might incorporate domain knowledge into a machine-learning NER engine and increase its accuracy.

Although many machine learning–based NER techniques require annotated data, semi-supervised and unsupervised techniques for NER have been long been explored due to their value in domain robustness and minimizing labor costs. Some attempts at automatic knowledgebase construction included automatic thesaurus discovery efforts (Grefenstette 1994), which sought to build lists of similar words without human intervention to aid in query expansion or automatic dictionary construction (Riloff 1996). More recently, the use of empirically derived semantics for NER is used by Finkel and Manning (Finkel and Manning 2009a), Turian et al. (Turian et al. 2010), and Jonnalagadda et al. (Siddhartha Jonnalagadda et al. 2010). Finkel's NER tool uses clusters of terms built apriori from the British National corpus (Aston and Burnard 1998) and English gigaword corpus (Graff et al. 2003) for extracting concepts from newswire text and PubMed abstracts for extracting gene mentions from biomedical literature. Turian et al. (Turian et al. 2010) also showed that statistically created word clusters (P. F. Brown et al. 1992; Clark 2000) could be used to improve named entity recognition. However, only a single feature (cluster membership) can be derived from the clusters. Semantic vector representations of terms had not been previously used for NER or sequential tagging classification tasks before (Turian et al. 2010). Although Jonnalagadda et al. (Siddhartha Jonnalagadda et al. 2010) use empirically derived vector representation for extracting concepts defined in the GENIA (Kim, Ohta, and Tsujii 2008) ontology from biomedical literature using rule-based methods, it was not clear whether such methods could be ported to extract other concepts or incrementally improve the performance of an existing system . This work not only demonstrates how such vector representation could improve state-of-the-art NER, but also that they are more useful than statistical clustering in this context.

Methods

We designed NER systems to identify treatment, tests, and medical problem entities in clinical notes and proteins in biomedical literature. Our systems are trained using 1) sentence-level features using training corpus; 2) a small lexicon created, compiled, and curated by humans for each domain; and 3) distributional semantics features derived from a large unannotated corpus of domain-relevant text. Different models are generated through different combinations of these features. After training for each concept class, a Conditional Random Field (CRF)-based machine-learning model is created to process input sentences using the same set of NLP features. The output is the set of sentences with the concepts tagged. We evaluated the performance of the different models in order to assess the degree to which human-curated lexicons can be substituted by the automatically created list of concepts.

Figure 1: Overall Architecture of the System

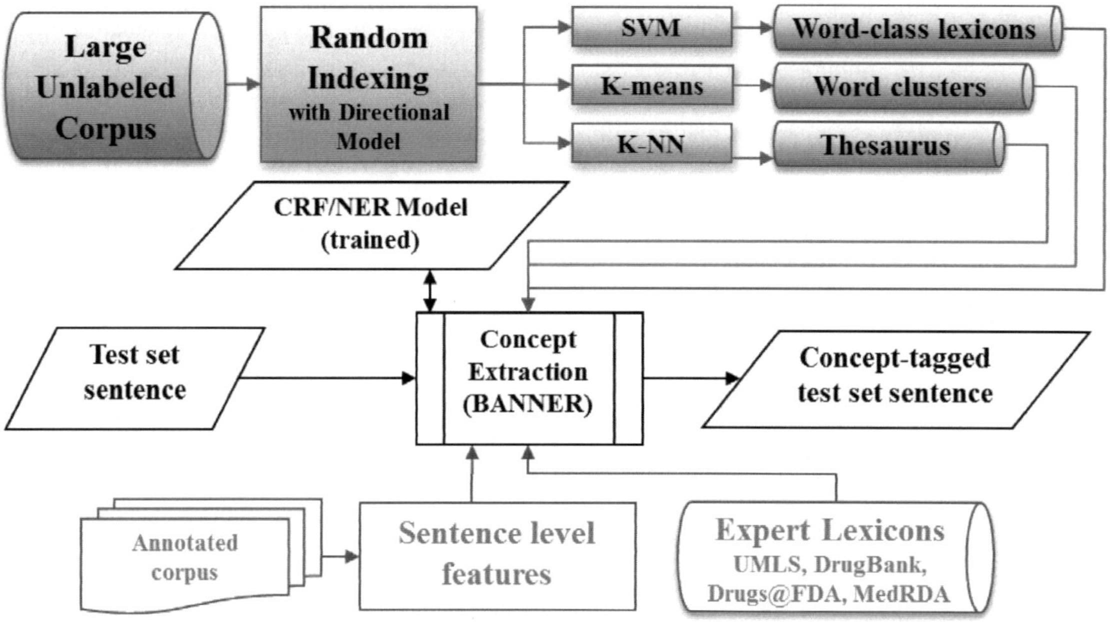

The design of the system to identify concepts using machine learning and distributional semantics. The top three components are related to distributional semantics.

The architecture of the system is shown in Figure 1. We first use a state-of-the-art NER algorithm, CRF, as implemented by MALLET (McCallum 2002), that extracts concepts from both clinical notes and biomedical literature using several orthographic and linguistic features derived from respective training corpora. Then, we study the impact on the performance of the baseline after incorporating manual lexical resources and empirically generated lexical resources. The CRF algorithm classifies words according to IOB or IO -like notations (I=inside, O=outside, B=beginning) to determine whether they are part of a description of an entity of interest, such as a treatment or protein. We used four labels for clinical NER— "Iproblem," "Itest," and "Itreatment," respectively, for tokens that were inside a problem, test, or treatment, and "O" if they were outside any clinical concept. For protein tagging, we used the IOB notation, i.e., there are three labels— "Iprotein," "Bprotein," and "O."

Several sentence-level orthographic and linguistic features such as lower-case tokens, lemmas, prefixes, suffixes, n-grams, patterns such as "beginning with a capital letter" and parts of speech are used by the systems to build the NER model and tag the entities in input sentences. This configuration is referred to as MED_noDict for clinical NER and BANNER_noDict for protein tagging.

The UMLS (Humphreys and Lindberg 1993), DrugBank (Wishart et al. 2006), Drugs@FDA (Food 2009), and MedDRA (E. G. Brown, Wood, and Wood 1999) are used to create dictionaries for medical problems, treatments and tests. The guidelines of the i2b2/VA NLP entity extraction task (i2b2 2010) are followed to identify the corresponding UMLS semantic types for each of the three concepts. The other three resources are used to add more terms to our manual lexicon. In an exhaustive evaluation on the nature of the resources by Gurulingappa et al. (Gurulingappa et al. 2010), UMLS and MedDRA were found to be the best resources for extracting information about medical problems among several other resources. For protein tagging, BANNER, one of the best protein-tagging systems (Kabiljo, Clegg, and Shepherd 2009), uses the 344,000 single-word lexicon constructed using the BioCreative II gene normalization training set (Morgan et al. 2008). This configuration is referred to as MED_Dict for clinical NER and as BANNER_Dict for protein tagging.

Distributional Semantic Feature Generation

Here, we implemented automatically generated distributional semantic features based on a semantic vector space model trained from unannotated corpora. This model, referred to as the directional model, uses a sliding window that is moved through the text corpus to generate a reduced-dimensional approximation of a token-token matrix, such that two terms that occur in the context of similar sets of surrounding terms will have similar vector representations after training. As the name suggests, the directional model takes into account the direction in which a word occurs with respect to another by generating a reduced-dimensional approximation of a matrix with two columns for each word, with one column representing the number of occurrences to the left and the other column representing the number of occurrences to the right. The directional model is therefore a form of sliding-window based Random Indexing (Kanerva, Kristoferson, and Holst 2000), and is related to the Hyperspace Analog to Language (Lund and Burgess 1996). Sliding-window Random Indexing models achieve dimension reduction by assigning a reduced-dimensional index vector to each term in a corpus. Index vectors are high dimensional (e.g. dimensionality on the order of 1,000), and are generated by randomly distributing a small number (e.g. on the order of 10) of +1's and -1's across this dimensionality. As the rest of the elements of the index vectors are 0, there is a high probability of index vectors being orthogonal, or close-to-orthogonal to one another. These index vectors are combined to generate context vectors representing the terms within a sliding window that is moved through the corpus. The semantic vector for a token is obtained by adding the contextual vectors gained at each occurrence of the token, which are derived from the index vectors for the other terms it occurs with in the sliding window. The model was built using the open source Semantic Vectors package (Widdows and Cohen 2010).

The performance of distributional models depends on the availability of an appropriate corpus of domain-relevant text. For clinical NER, 447,000 Medline abstracts that are indexed as pertaining to clinical trials are used as the unlabeled corpus. In addition, we have also used clinical notes from Mayo Clinic and University of Texas Health Science Center to understand the impact of the source of unlabeled corpus. For protein NER, 8,955,530 Medline citations in the 2008 baseline release that include an abstract (2010) are used as the large unlabeled corpus. Previous experiments (Siddhartha Jonnalagadda et al. 2012) revealed that using 2000-dimensional vectors, five seeds (number of +1s and –1s in the vector), and a window radius of six is better suited for the task of NER. While a stop-word list is not employed, we have rejected tokens that appear only once in the unlabeled corpus or have more than three nonalphabetical characters.

Quasi-Lexicons of Concept Classes Using SVM

SVM (Cortes and Vapnik 1995) is designed to draw hyper-planes separating two class regions such that they have a maximum margin of separation. Creating the quasi-lexicons (automatically generated word lists) is equivalent to obtaining samples of regions in the distributional hyperspace that contain tokens from the desired (problem, treatment, test and none) semantic types. In clinical NER, each token in training set can belong to either one or more of the classes: problem, treatment, test, or none of these. Each token is labeled as "Iproblem," "Itest," "Itreatment" or "Inone." To remove ambiguity, tokens that belong to more than one category are discarded. Each token has a representation in the distributional hyperspace of 2,000 dimensions. Six (C[4, 2] = 4!/[2!*2!]) binary SVM classifiers are generated for predicting the class of any token among the four possible categories. During the execution of the training and testing phase of the CRF machine-learning algorithm, the class predicted by the SVM classifiers for each token is used as a feature for that token.

Clusters of Distributionally Similar Words Over K-Means
The K-means clustering algorithm (MacQueen 1967) is used to group the tokens in the training corpus into 200 clusters using distributional semantic vectors. The cluster identifier assigned to the target token is used as a feature for the CRF-based system for NER. This feature is similar to the Clark's automatically created clusters (Clark 2000), used by Finkel and Manning (Finkel and Manning 2009b), where the same number of clusters are used. We focused on using features generated from *semantic vectors* as they allow us to also create the other two types of features.

Quasi-Thesaurus of Distributionally Similar Words Using N-Nearest Neighbors
Figure 2: Nearest Tokens to Haloperidol

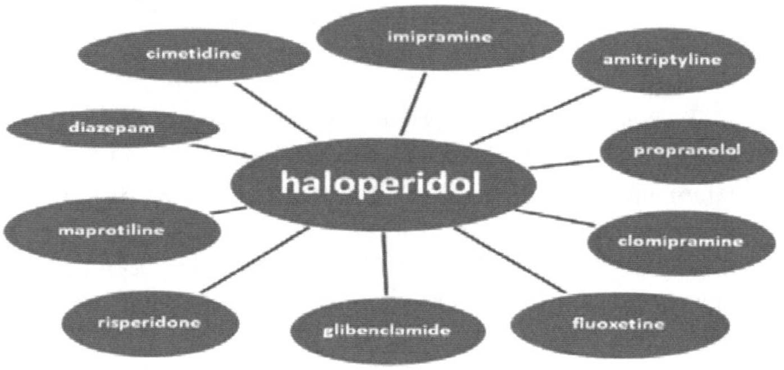

The closest tokens to haloperidol in the word space are psychiatric drugs. Using the nearest tokens to haloperidol as features, when haloperidol is not a manually compiled lexicon or when the context is unclear, would help to still infer (statistically) that haloperidol is a drug (medical treatment).

Cosine similarity of vectors is used to find the 20 nearest tokens for each token. These nearest tokens are used as features for the respective target token. Figure 2 shows the top few tokens closest in the word space to "haloperidol" to demonstrate how well the semantic vectors are computed. Each of these nearest tokens is used as an additional feature whenever the target token is encountered. Barring evidence from other features, the word "haloperidol" would be classified as belonging to the "medical treatment," "drug," or "psychiatric drug" semantic class based on other words belonging to that class sharing nearest neighbors with it.

Evaluation Strategy
The previous sub-sections detail how the manually created lexicons are compiled and how the empirical lexical resources are generated from semantic vectors (2000 dimensions). In the respective machine learning system for extracting concepts from literature and clinical notes, each manually created lexicon (three for the clinical notes task) contributes one binary feature whose value depends on whether a term surrounding the word is present in the lexicon. Each quasi-lexicon will also contribute one binary feature whose value depends on the output of the SVM classifier discussed before. The distributional semantic clusters together contribute a feature whole value is the id of the cluster the word belongs to. The quasi-thesaurus contributes 20 features that are the 20 distributionally similar words to the word for which features are being generated.

As a gold standard for clinical NER, the fourth i2b2/VA NLP shared-task corpus (i2b2 2010) for extracting concepts of the classes—problems, treatments, and tests—is used. The corpus contains 349 clinical notes as training data and 477 clinical notes as testing data. For protein tagging, the BioCreative II Gene Mention Task (Wilbur, Smith, and Tanabe 2007) corpus is used. The corpus contains 15,000 training set sentences and 5,000 testing set sentences.

Results

Comparison of Different Types of Lexical Resources on Extracting Clinical Concepts

Table 1: Clinical NER: Comparison of SVM-Based Features and Clustering-Based Features With N-Nearest Neighbors–Based Features

Setting	Exact F	Inexact F	Exact Increase	Inexact Increase
MED_Dict	80.3	89.7		
MED_Dict+SVM	80.6	90	0.3	0.3
MED_Dict+NN	81.7	90.9	1.4	1.2
MED_Dict+NN+SVM	81.9	91	1.6	1.3
MED_Dict+CL	80.8	90.1	0.5	0.4
MED_Dict+NN+SVM+CL	81.7	90.9	1.4	1.2

MED_Dict is the baseline, which is a machine-learning clinical NER system with several orthographic and syntactic features, along with features from lexicons such as UMLS, Drugs@FDA, and MedDRA. In MED_Dict+SVM, the quasi-lexicons are also used. In MED_Dict+NN, the quasi-thesaurus is used. In MED_Dict+CL, the clusters automatically generated are used in addition to other features in MED_Dict. Exact F is the F-score for exact match as calculated by the shared task software. Inexact F is the F-score for inexact match or matcing only a part of the other. Exact Increase is the increase in Exact F from previous row. Inexact Increase is the increase in Inexact F from previous row.

Table 1 shows that the F-score of the clinical NER system for exact match increases by 0.3% after adding quasi-lexicons, whereas it increases by 1.4% after adding quasi-thesaurus. The F-score slightly increases further with the use of both these features. The F-score for an inexact match follows a similar pattern. Table 1 also shows that the F-score for an exact match increases by 0.5% after adding clustering-based features, whereas it increases by 1.6% after adding quasi-thesaurus and quasi-lexicons. The F-score slightly decreases with the use of both the features. The F-score for an inexact match follows a similar pattern.

Overall Impact on Extracting Clinical Concepts

Table 2: Clinical NER: Impact of Distributional Semantic Features

Setting	Exact F	Inexact F	Exact Increase	Inexact Increase
MED_noDict	79.4	89.2		
MED_Dict	80.3	89.7	0.9	0.5
MED_noDict+NN+SVM	81.4	90.8	2.0	1.6
MED_Dict+NN+SVM	81.9	91.0	2.5	1.8

MED_noDict is the machine-learning clinical NER system with all the orthographic and syntactic features, but no features from lexicons such as UMLS, Drugs@FDA, and MedDRA. MED_noDict+NN+SVM also has the features generated using SVM and the nearest neighbors algorithm.

Table 2 shows how the F-score increased over the baseline (MED_noDict, which uses various orthographic and syntactic features). After manually constructed lexicon features are added (MED_Dict), it increased by 0.9%. On the other hand, if only distributional semantic features (quasi-thesaurus and quasi-lexicons) were added without using manually constructed lexicon features (MED_noDict+NN+SVM), it increased by 2.0% ($P<0.001$ using Bootstrap Resampling (Noreen 1989) with 1,000 repetitions). It increases only by 0.5% more if the manually constructed lexicon features were used along with distributional semantic features (MED_Dict+NN+SVM). The F-score for an inexact match follows a similar pattern.

Moreover, Table 3 shows that the improvement is consistent even across different concept classes, namely medical problems, tests, and treatments. Each time the distributional semantic features are added, the number of TPs increases, the number of FPs decreases, and the number of FNs decreases.

Impact of the Source of the Unlabeled Data

We utilized three sources for creating the distributional semantics models for NER from i2b2/VA clinical notes corpus. The first source is the set of Medline abstracts indexed as pertaining to clinical trials (447,000 in the 2010 baseline). The second source is the set of 0.8 million clinical notes (half of the total available) from the clinical data warehouse at the School of Biomedical Informatics, University of Texas Health Sciences Center, Houston, Texas (http://www.uthouston.edu/uth-big/clinical-data-warehouse.htm). The third source is the set of 0.8 million randomly chosen clinical notes written by clinicians at Mayo Clinic in Rochester. Table 3 shows the performance of the systems that use each of these sources for creating the distributional semantics features. Each of these systems has a significantly higher F-score than the system that does not use any distributional semantic feature (*P*<0.001 using Bootstrap Resampling (Noreen 1989) with 1,000 repetitions and a difference in F-score of 2.0%). The F-scores of these systems are almost the same (differing by <0.5%).

Table 3: Clinical NER: Impact of the Source of Unlabeled Corpus

Unlabeled Corpus	Exact F	Inexact F
None	80.3	89.7
Medline	81.9	91.0
UT Houston	82.3	91.3
Mayo	82.0	91.3

None = The machine-learning clinical NER system that does not use any distributional semantic features. Medline = The machine-learning clinical NER system that uses distributional semantic features derived from the Medline abstracts indexed as pertaining to clinical trials. UT Houston = The machine-learning clinical NER system that uses distributional semantic features derived from the notes in the clinical data warehouse at University of Texas Health Sciences Center. Mayo = The machine-learning clinical NER system that uses distributional semantic features derived from the clinical notes of Mayo Clinic, Rochester, MN.

Impact of the Size of the Unlabeled Data

Using the set of 1.6 million clinical notes from the clinical data warehouse at the University of Texas Health Sciences Center as the baseline, we studied the relationship between the size of the unlabeled corpus used and the accuracy achieved. We randomly created subsets of size one-half, one-fourth, and one-eighth the original corpus and measured the respective F-scores. Figure 3 depicts the F-score for exact match and inexact match, suggesting a monotonic relationship with the number of documents used for creating the distributional semantic measures. While there is a leap from not using any unlabeled corpus to using 0.2 million clinical notes, the F-score is relatively constant from there. We might infer that by incrementally adding more documents to the unlabeled corpus, one would be able to determine what size of corpus is sufficient.

Figure 3: Impact of the Size of the Unlabeled Corpus

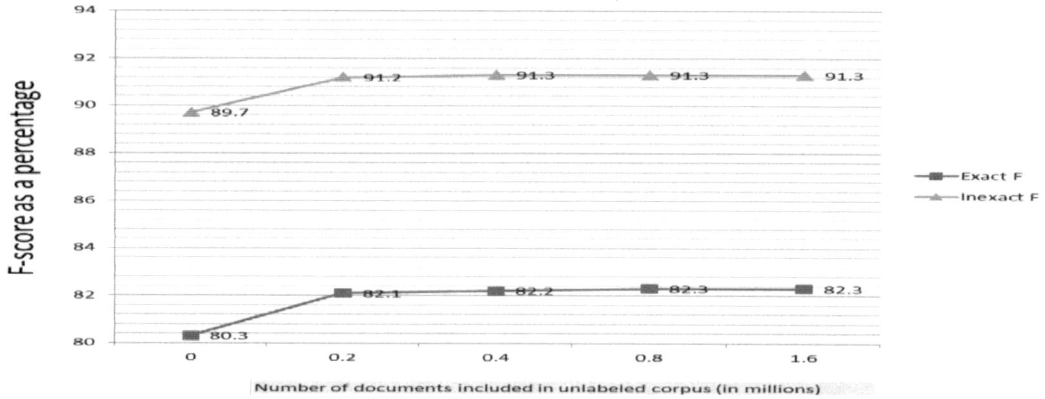

On the X-axis, N represents the system created using distributional semantic features from N-unlabeled documents. N=0 refers to the system that does not use any distributional semantic feature.

Impact on Extracting Protein Mentions

Table 4: Protein Tagging: Impact of Distributional Semantic Features on BANNER

Rank	Setting	Precision	Recall	F-score	Significance
1	Rank 1 system	88.48	85.97	87.21	6-11
2	Rank 2 system	89.30	84.49	86.83	8-11
3	BANNER_Dict+DistSem	88.25	85.12	86.66	8-11
4	Rank 3 system	84.93	88.28	86.57	8-11
5	BANNER_noDict+DistSem	87.95	85.06	86.48	10-11
6	Rank 4 system	87.27	85.41	86.33	10-11
7	Rank 5 system	85.77	86.80	86.28	10-11
8	Rank 6 system	82.71	89.32	85.89	10-11
9	BANNER_Dict	86.41	84.55	85.47	-
10	Rank 7 system	86.97	82.55	84.70	-
11	BANNER_noDict	85.63	83.10	84.35	-

The significance column indicates which systems are significantly less accurate than the system in the corresponding row. These values are based on the Bootstrap re-sampling calculations performed as part of the evaluation in the BioCreative II shared task (the latest gene or protein tagging task). BANNER_Dict+DistSem is the system that uses both manual and empirical lexical resources. BANNER_noDict+DistSem is the system that uses only empirical lexical resources. BANNER_Dict is the system that uses only manual lexical resources. This is the system available prior to this research, and the baseline for this study. BANNER_noDict is the system that uses neither manual nor empirical lexical resources. BANNER_Dict+DistSem is the system that is significantly more accurate than the baseline. It is equally important to the improvement that the accuracy of BANNER_noDict+DistSem is better than BANNER_noDict. The most significant contribution in terms of research is that an equivalent accuracy (BANNER_noDict+DistSem and BANNER_Dict) could be achieved even without using any manually compiled lexical resources apart from the annotated corpora.

In Table 4, the performance of BANNER with distributional semantic features (row 3) and without distributional semantic features (row 9) is compared with the top ranking systems in the most recent gene-mention task of the BioCreative shared tasks. Each system has an F-score that has a statistically significant comparison ($P<0.05$) with the teams indicated in the *Significance* column. The significance is estimated using Table 1 in the BioCreative II gene mention task (Wilbur, Smith, and Tanabe 2007). The performance of BANNER with distributional semantic features and no manually constructed lexicon features is better than BANNER with manually constructed lexicon features and no distributional semantic features. This demonstrates again that distributional semantic features (that are generated automatically) are more useful than manually constructed lexicon features (that are usually compiled and cleaned manually) as means to enhance supervised machine learning for NER.

Discussion

The evaluations for clinical NER reveal that the distributional semantic features are better than manually constructed lexicon features. The accuracy further increases when both manually created dictionaries and distributional semantic feature types are used, but the increase is not very significant (P=0.15 using Bootstrap Resampling (Noreen 1989) with 1,000 repetitions). This shows that distributional semantic features could supplement manually built lexicons, but the development of the lexicon, if it does not exist, might not be as critical as previously believed. Further, the N-nearest neighbor (quasi-thesaurus) features are better than SVM-based (quasi-lexicons) features and clustering-based (quasi-clusters) features for improving the accuracy of clinical NER ($P<0.001$ using Bootstrap Resampling (Noreen 1989) with 1,000 repetitions). For the protein extraction task, the improvement after adding the distributional semantic features to BANNER is also significant ($P<0.001$ using Bootstrap Resampling (Noreen 1989) with 1,000 repetitions). The absolute ranking of

BANNER with respect to other systems in the BioCreative II task improves from 8 to 3. The F-score of the best system is not significantly better than that of BANNER with distributional semantic features. We again notice that distributional semantic features are more useful than manually constructed lexicon features alone. The purpose of using protein mention extraction in addition to NER from clinical notes is to verify that the methods are generalizable. Hence, we only used the nearest neighbor or quasi-thesaurus features (as the other features contributed little) for protein mention extraction and have not studied the impact of the source or size of the unlabeled data separately. The advantages of our features are that they are independent of the machine-learning system used and can be used to further improve the performance of forthcoming algorithms.

The increment in F-scores after adding manually compiled dictionaries (without distributional semantic features) is only around 1%. However, many NER tools, both in the genomic domain (Leaman and Gonzalez 2008; Torii et al. 2009) and in the clinical domain (Friedman 1997; Savova et al. 2010) use dictionaries. This is partly because systems trained using supervised machine-learning algorithms are often sensitive to the distribution of data, and a model trained on one corpus may perform poorly on those trained from another. For example, Wagholikar (Wagholikar et al. 2012) recently showed that a machine-learning model for NER trained on the i2b2/VA corpus achieved a significantly lower F-score when tested on the Mayo Clinic corpus. Other researchers recently reported this phenomenon for part of speech tagging in clinical domain (Fan et al. 2011). A similar observation was made for the protein-named entity extraction using the GENIA, GENETAG, and AIMED corpora (Wang et al. 2009; Ohta et al. 2009), as well as for protein-protein interaction extraction using the GENIA and AIMED corpora (Siddhartha Jonnalagadda and Gonzalez 2010; S. Jonnalagadda and Gonzalez 2009). The domain knowledge gathered through these semantic features might make the system less sensitive. This work showed that empirically gained semantics are at least as useful for NER as the manually compiled dictionaries. It would be interesting to see if such a drastic decline in performance across different corpora could be countered using distributional semantic features.

Currently, very little difference is observed between using distributional semantic features derived from Medline and unlabeled clinical notes for the task of clinical NER. In the future, we would study the impact using clinical notes related to a specific specialty of medicine. We hypothesize that the distributional semantic features from clinical notes of a subspecialty might be more useful than the corresponding literature. Our current results lack qualitative evaluation. As we repeat the experiments in a subspecialty such as cardiology, we would be able to involve the domain experts in the qualitative analysis of the distributional semantic features and their role in the NER.

Conclusion

Our evaluations using clinical notes and biomedical literature validate that distributional semantic features are useful to obtain domain information automatically, irrespective of the domain, and can reduce the need to create, compile, and clean dictionaries, thereby facilitating the efficient adaptation of NER systems to new application domains. We showed this through analyzing results for NER of four different classes (genes, medical problems, tests, and treatments) of concepts in two domains (biomedical literature and clinical notes). Though the combination of manually constructed lexicon features and distributional semantic features has slightly better performance, suggesting that if a manually constructed lexicon is available, it should be used, the de-novo creation of a lexicon for purpose of NER is not needed.

The distributional semantics model for Medline and the quasi-thesaurus prepared from the i2b2/VA corpus and the clinical NER system's code is available at (http://diego.asu.edu/downloads/AZCCE/) and the updates to the BANNER system are incorporated at http://banner.sourceforge.net/.

Acknowledgments

This work was possible because of funding from possible sources: NLM HHSN276201000031C (PI: Gonzalez), NCRR 3UL1RR024148, NCRR 1RC1RR028254, NSF 0964613 and the Brown Foundation (PI: Bernstam), NSF ABI:0845523, NLM R01LM009959A1 (PI: Liu) and NLM 1K99LM011389 (PI: Jonnalagadda). We also thank the developers of BANNER (http://banner.sourceforge.net/), MALLET (http://mallet.cs.umass.edu/) and Semantic Vectors (http://code.google.com/p/semanticvectors/) for the software packages and the organizers of the i2b2/VA 2010 NLP challenge for sharing the corpus.

References

Aston, G., and L. Burnard. 1998. *The BNC Handbook: Exploring the British National Corpus with SARA*. Edinburgh Univ Pr.

Brown, E G, L Wood, and S Wood. 1999. "The Medical Dictionary for Regulatory Activities (MedDRA)." *Drug Safety: An International Journal of Medical Toxicology and Drug Experience* 20 (2) (February): 109–117.

Brown, P. F, P. V Desouza, R. L Mercer, V. J.D Pietra, and J. C Lai. 1992. "Class-based N-gram Models of Natural Language." *Computational Linguistics* 18 (4): 467–479.

Clark, A. 2000. "Inducing Syntactic Categories by Context Distribution Clustering." In *Proceedings of the 2nd Workshop on Learning Language in Logic and the 4th Conference on Computational Natural Language learning-Volume 7*, 91–94. Association for Computational Linguistics Morristown, NJ, USA.

Cortes, C., and V. Vapnik. 1995. "Support-Vector Networks." *Machine Learning* 20: 273–297.

Fan, Jung-wei, Rashmi Prasad, Rommel M Yabut, Richard M Loomis, Daniel S Zisook, John E Mattison, and Yang Huang. 2011. "Part-of-speech Tagging for Clinical Text: Wall or Bridge Between Institutions?" *AMIA ... Annual Symposium Proceedings / AMIA Symposium. AMIA Symposium* 2011: 382–391.

Finkel, J. R., and C. D. Manning. 2009a. "Joint Parsing and Named Entity Recognition." In *Proceedings of Human Language Technologies: The 2009 Annual Conference of the North American Chapter of the Association for Computational Linguistics on ZZZ*, 326–334. Association for Computational Linguistics.

———. 2009b. "Nested Named Entity Recognition." In *Proceedings of the 2009 Conference on Empirical Methods in Natural Language Processing*.

Food, U. S. 2009. "Drug Administration. Drugs@ FDA." *FDA Approved Drug Products*. http://www.accessdata.fda. gov/scripts/cder/drugsatfda.

Friedman, Carol. 1997. "Towards a Comprehensive Medical Language Processing System: Methods and Issues." In *AMIA*.

Graff, D., J. Kong, K. Chen, and K. Maeda. 2003. "English Gigaword." *Linguistic Data Consortium, Philadelphia*.

Grefenstette, Gregory. 1994. *Explorations in Automatic Thesaurus Discovery*. Norwell, MA, USA: Kluwer Academic Publishers.

Gurulingappa, H., R. Klinger, M. Hofmann-Apitius, and J. Fluck. 2010. "An Empirical Evaluation of Resources for the Identification of Diseases and Adverse Effects in Biomedical Literature." In *2nd Workshop on Building and Evaluating Resources for Biomedical Text Mining*, 15.

Humphreys, B L, and D A Lindberg. 1993. "The UMLS Project: Making the Conceptual Connection Between Users and the Information They Need." *Bulletin of the Medical Library Association* 81 (2) (April): 170–177.

i2b2. 2010. "Fourth i2b2/VA Shared-Task and Workshop." *Fourth i2b2/VA Shared-Task and Workshop*. https://www.i2b2.org/NLP/Relations.

Jonnalagadda, S., and G. Gonzalez. 2009. "Sentence Simplification Aids Protein-Protein Interaction Extraction." In *Languages in Biology and Medicine*.

Jonnalagadda, Siddhartha, Trevor Cohen, Stephen Wu, and Graciela Gonzalez. 2012. "Enhancing Clinical Concept Extraction with Distributional Semantics." *Journal of Biomedical Informatics* 45 (1) (February): 129–140. doi:10.1016/j.jbi.2011.10.007.

Jonnalagadda, Siddhartha, and Graciela Gonzalez. 2010. "BioSimplify: An Open Source Sentence Simplification Engine to Improve Recall in Automatic Biomedical Information Extraction." In *AMIA Annual Symposium Proceedings*.

Jonnalagadda, Siddhartha, Robert Leaman, Trevor Cohen, and Graciela Gonzalez. 2010. "A Distributional Semantics Approach to Simultaneous Recognition of Multiple Classes of

Named Entities." In *Computational Linguistics and Intelligent Text Processing (CICLing)*. Vol. 6008/2010. Lecture Notes in Computer Science.
Kabiljo, R., A. B Clegg, and A. J Shepherd. 2009. "A Realistic Assessment of Methods for Extracting Gene/protein Interactions from Free Text." *BMC Bioinformatics* 10: 233.
Kanerva, P., J. Kristoferson, and A. Holst. 2000. "Random Indexing of Text Samples for Latent Semantic Analysis." In *Proceedings of the 22nd Annual Conference of the Cognitive Science Society*. Vol. 1036.
Kim, J. D., T. Ohta, and J. Tsujii. 2008. "Corpus Annotation for Mining Biomedical Events from Literature." *BMC Bioinformatics* 9 (January 8): 10.
Leaman, R., and G. Gonzalez. 2008. "BANNER: An Executable Survey of Advances in Biomedical Named Entity Recognition." In *Pacific Symposium in Bioinformatics*.
Lund, K., and C. Burgess. 1996. "Hyperspace Analog to Language (HAL): A General Model of Semantic Representation." *Language and Cognitive Processes*.
MacQueen, J. 1967. "Some Methods for Classification and Analysis of Multivariate Observations." In *Proceedings of 5th Berkeley Symposium on Mathematical Statistics and Probability*.
McCallum, AK. 2002. "MALLET: A Machine Learning for Language Toolkit." http://mallet.cs.umass.edu.
Morgan, A., Z. Lu, X. Wang, A. Cohen, J. Fluck, P. Ruch, A. Divoli, K. Fundel, R. Leaman, and J. Hakenberg. 2008. "Overview of BioCreative II Gene Normalization." *Genome Biology* 9 (Suppl 2): S3.
NLM. 2010. "MEDLINE®/PubMed® Baseline Statistics." http://www.nlm.nih.gov/bsd/licensee/baselinestats.html.
Noreen, E. W. 1989. *Computer-intensive Methods for Testing Hypotheses: An Introduction*. New York: John Wiley & Sons, Inc.
Ohta, Tomoko, Jin-Dong Kim, Sampo Pyysalo, Yue Wang, and Jun'ichi Tsujii. 2009. "Incorporating GENETAG-style Annotation to GENIA Corpus." In *Proceedings of the Workshop on Current Trends in Biomedical Natural Language Processing*, 106–107. BioNLP '09. Stroudsburg, PA, USA: Association for Computational Linguistics. http://portal.acm.org/citation.cfm?id=1572364.1572379.
Riloff, Ellen. 1996. "An Empirical Study of Automated Dictionary Construction for Information Extraction in Three Domains." *Artif. Intell.* 85 (1-2) (August): 101–134. doi:10.1016/0004-3702(95)00123-9.
Savova, G. K., J. J. Masanz, P. V. Ogren, J. Zheng, S. Sohn, K. C. Kipper-Schuler, and C. G. Chute. 2010. "Mayo Clinical Text Analysis and Knowledge Extraction System (cTAKES): Architecture, Component Evaluation and Applications." *Journal of the American Medical Informatics Association* 17 (5) (September): 507–513. doi:10.1136/jamia.2009.001560.
Stanfill, Mary H, Margaret Williams, Susan H Fenton, Robert A Jenders, and William R Hersh. 2010. "A Systematic Literature Review of Automated Clinical Coding and Classification Systems." *Journal of the American Medical Informatics Association: JAMIA* 17 (6) (November 1): 646–651. doi:10.1136/jamia.2009.001024.
Torii, M., Z. Hu, C. H. Wu, and H. Liu. 2009. "BioTagger-GM: A Gene/protein Name Recognition System." *Journal of the American Medical Informatics Association* 16 (2): 247–255.
Turian, J., R. Opérationnelle, L. Ratinov, and Y. Bengio. 2010. "Word Representations: A Simple and General Method for Semi-supervised Learning." In *ACL*, 51:61801.
Wagholikar, Kavishwar, Manabu Torii, Siddhartha Jonnala, and Hongfang Liu. 2012. "Feasibility of Pooling Annotated Corpora for Clinical Concept Extraction." In Vol. Accepted for publication.
Wang, Yue, Jin-Dong Kim, Rune Sætre, Sampo Pyysalo, and Jun'ichi Tsujii. 2009. "Investigating Heterogeneous Protein Annotations Toward Cross-corpora Utilization." *BMC Bioinformatics* 10 (1): 403. doi:10.1186/1471-2105-10-403.
Widdows, D., and T. Cohen. 2010. "The Semantic Vectors Package: New Algorithms and Public Tools for Distributional Semantics." In *Fourth IEEE International Conference on Semantic Computing*, 1:43.
Wilbur, J., L. Smith, and T. Tanabe. 2007. "BioCreative 2 Gene Mention Task." *Proceedings of the Second BioCreative Challenge Workshop* 7-16.

Wishart, David S, Craig Knox, An Chi Guo, Savita Shrivastava, Murtaza Hassanali, Paul Stothard, Zhan Chang, and Jennifer Woolsey. 2006. "DrugBank: a Comprehensive Resource for in Silico Drug Discovery and Exploration." *Nucleic Acids Research* 34 (Database issue) (January 1): D668–672. doi:10.1093/nar/gkj067.

Towards Converting Clinical Phrases into SNOMED CT Expressions

Rohit J. Kate
University of Wisconsin-Milwaukee
katerj@uwm.edu

Abstract

Converting information contained in natural language clinical text into computer-amenable structured representations can automate many clinical applications. As a step towards that goal, we present a method which could help in converting novel clinical phrases into new expressions in SNOMED CT, a standard clinical terminology. Since expressions in SNOMED CT are written in terms of their relations with other SNOMED CT concepts, we formulate the important task of identifying relations between clinical phrases and SNOMED CT concepts. We present a machine learning approach for this task and using the dataset of existing SNOMED CT relations we show that it performs well.

1 Introduction

Many clinical applications, including clinical decision support, medical error detection, answering clinical queries, generating patient statistics, and biosurveillance, would be automated if the clinical information locked in natural language clinical text could be converted into computer-amenable structured representations. To enable this, a long-term goal is to convert entire natural language clinical documents into structured representations. As an important step in that direction, in this paper we focus on a task that can help in converting clinical phrases into a structured representation. SNOMED CT (IHTSDO, 2009) is a standardized representation for clinical concepts whose extensiveness and expressivity makes it suitable for precisely encoding clinical phrases. A concept in SNOMED CT is defined in terms of its relations with other concepts and it currently includes around four hundred thousand pre-defined clinical concepts. If a natural language clinical phrase represents a concept which is already present in SNOMED CT then the conversion process reduces to a matching function; some previous work (Stenzhorn et al., 2009; Barrett et al., 2012) as well as existing SNOMED CT browsers, like CliniClue,[1] can automatically perform such a matching. But our focus in this paper is instead on the task of creating new SNOMED CT concepts for clinical phrases for which no SNOMED CT concept already exists.

Since new concepts in SNOMED CT can be created by identifying their relations with existing SNOMED CT concepts, we formulate the important task of identifying relations between clinical phrases and SNOMED CT concepts. That is, given a clinical phrase (for example, "acute gastric ulcer with perforation") and a description of a SNOMED CT concept (for example, "stomach structure"), whether a particular kind of relation (for example, "finding site") is present between them or not (in this example it is present). To the best of our knowledge, there is no other work which has attempted this type of relation identification task. Note that this task is very different from the relation extraction task (Zelenko et al., 2003). In that task, two entities are given in a sentence and the system determines whether the two entities are related or not mostly based on what the sentence says. In contrast, there is no sentence in this task and the presence of a relation is determined entirely based on the two entities.

Since several thousand relations already exist in SNOMED CT, we used these existing relations to form our dataset. Both training and test relation example pairs were obtained from this dataset. To identify each kind of relation we separately trained a machine learning method. We employed SVM

[1] http://www.cliniclue.com

(Cristianini and Shawe-Taylor, 2000) machine learning method in combination with a new kernel that we specifically designed for this relation identification task. The experimental results show that the trained system obtains a good accuracy.

Such a system could be used for creating precise SNOMED CT expressions for clinical phrases. For example, “acute gastric ulcer with perforation” could be represented as an “acute gastric ulcer”, whose finding site is “stomach structure” and whose associated morphologies are “perforated ulcer” and “acute ulcer” (this is also shown in Table 1 under phrase (c)). In this example, “is a”, “finding site” and “associated morphology” are the identified relations, and “acute gastric ulcer”, “stomach structure”, “perforated ulcer” and “acute ulcer” are already present concepts in SNOMED CT. This representation would be obtained by efficiently testing the phrase for all the relations and with all the existing SNOMED CT concepts.

2 Background and Related Work

Realizing the importance of unlocking the clinical information present in free-text clinical reports, researchers started working on automatically converting them into structured representations years ago. Previous systems to convert natural language clinical information into structured representation, like LSP (Sager et al., 1987, 1995), MedLEE (Friedman et al., 1994, 2004) and Menelas (Spyns et al., 1992; Spyns and Willems, 1995), were manually built by linguistically and medically trained experts over a long course of time. The builders manually encoded how different natural language patterns should convert into the target structured representations. They also developed their own suitable structured representations (Friedman et al., 1993; Zweigenbaum et al., 1995) which restricts their systems from being useful elsewhere where a different type of structured representation is in use. Although we are limiting ourselves to clinical phrases instead of full sentences at this stage, we use machine learning techniques to minimize the manual cost of building such a system. For the structured representation, we are using the standardized clinical terminology, SNOMED CT, which is already widely in use.

Systematized Nomenclature of Medicine - Clinical Terms (SNOMED CT; IHTSDO, 2009) is the most comprehensive clinical terminology in the world today and is widely used in electronic health record systems for documentation purposes and reporting (Benson, 2010). Its extensive content and expressivity makes it suitable for precisely encoding clinical concepts. Not only does it specify around four hundred thousand pre-defined medical concepts and relations between them, but also its compositional grammar (IHTSDO, 2008) can be used to build new expressions that represent new medical concepts in terms of the existing concepts. SNOMED CT has been developed in the description logic formalism (Baader et al., 2003) which also makes it suitable for automated reasoning. For all these reasons, we think that it is the best structured representation into which natural language clinical phrases may be converted. There are browsers and tools available that can help users search SNOMED CT as well as interactively build new expressions, like CliniClue. Lee et al. (2010) presented a method for manually encoding text with SNOMED CT. There also has been recent work in automatically mapping text to SNOMED CT pre-defined concepts (Jung et al., 2009; Stenzhorn et al., 2009; Barrett et al., 2012) or UMLS pre-defined concepts (Aronson and Lang, 2010). However, these systems at best do an approximate match from clinical phrases to pre-defined concepts, also known as *pre-coordinated expressions*. In contrast, the system presented in this paper can help to automatically map natural language clinical phrases which do not match any pre-defined concepts into their semantically equivalent new SNOMED CT expressions. The new SNOMED CT expressions are also known as *post-coordinated expressions*. We did a preliminary analysis of the i2b2 2010 clinical text corpus (Uzuner et al., 2011) and found that out of around 8300 unique annotated concepts (noun phrases) in it, only around 1600 were pre-defined concepts in SNOMED CT. This shows that new phrases are abundantly present in clinical text and hence the ability to convert them into new SNOMED CT expressions is important.

Natural Language Clinical Phrase	SNOMED CT Expresesion
(a) severe pain in the stomach	116680003 |is a| = 22253000 |pain| {363698007 |finding site| = 69695003 | stomach structure |, 272141005 |severity| = 24484000 |severe| }
(b) neoplasm of right lower lobe of lung	116680003 |is a| = 126713003 |neoplasm of lung| {116676008 |associated morphology| = 108369006 |neoplasm|, 363698007 |finding site| = 266005 |structure of right lower lobe of lung|}
(c) acute gastric ulcer with perforation	116680003 |is a| = 95529005 |acute gastric ulcer| {363698007 |finding site| = 69695003 | stomach structure |, 116676008 |associated morphology| = 26317001 |acute ulcer|, 116676008 |associated morphology| = 91182001 |perforated ulcer|}
(d) family history of aplastic anemia	116680003 |is a| 243796009 |situation with explicit context| {246090004 |associated finding| = 306058006 |aplastic anemia| {408732007 |subject relationship context| = 303071001 |person in the family|} }

Table 1: Some examples of natural language clinical phrases and their corresponding SNOMED CT expressions. The numbers are the SNOMED CT concept and relation identifiers and their natural language descriptions are shown for human readability. The "=" character indicates relation kind on its left side and the related concept on its right side.

3 Identifying SNOMED CT Relations

3.1 Formulation of the Task

Table 1 shows some examples of clinical phrases and their associated SNOMED CT expressions. The expressions are shown using the syntax of SNOMED CT's compositional grammar (IHTSDO, 2008). The numbers are the unique SNOMED CT concept and relation identifiers. Each concept in SNOMED CT has at least one natural language description. A description for each concept and relation is shown within vertical bars for human readability. The "=" character denotes relation kind on its left side and the related concept on its right side. The "is a" relation identifies the basic concept a clinical phrase represents and this is then further qualified using more relations which are shown in "{}" brackets. Note that there could be multiple relations of the same kind in an expression, for example, in phrase (c) the "associated morphology" relation occurs twice. Similarly, even the "is a" relation can occur more than once because SNOMED CT allows multiple inheritance of concepts. There is more than one way to write an expression in SNOMED CT, ranging from close-to-user form to normal form (IHTSDO, 2009). We have shown close-to-user forms in the Table 1 which are simpler and easier for humans to understand. For the record, the concepts for phrases (b) and (c) are already present in the current version of SNOMED CT but the concepts for phrases (a) and (d) are not present.

As it can be observed, relations are the basis for forming SNOMED CT expressions. Hence, in this paper, we formulate the task of identifying relations between clinical phrases and SNOMED CT concepts. A new SNOMED CT expression could then be formed for a new clinical phrase by identifying its relations with exiting concepts. We present a machine learning method for training a separate relation identifier for each of the relations present in SNOMED CT (for example, "is a", "finding site" etc.). Since every concept in SNOMED CT has a basic type (for example, "substance", "disorder", "body structure" etc.), and the basic type can also be determined for every clinical phrase (either directly from the context it is used in or by using a trained classifier),[2] we treat each relation with different types separately. For

[2]Alternatively, the type of a clinical phrase could also be identified by first determining the "is_a" relation.

example, the "finding site" relation that relates "disorder" to "body structure" is treated separately from the "finding site" relation that relates "finding" to "body structure". The first column of Table 2 shows the most frequent relations in SNOMED CT along with their types which we used in our experiments.

Since several hundred thousand concepts and the relations between them are already present in SNOMED CT, we decided to use them as our dataset for training and testing our method. Every concept in SNOMED CT has a unique identifier and is also given a unique fully specified natural language name. In addition, it may have several natural language descriptions which are essentially a few different ways of expressing the same concept. To create our dataset, for every kind of relation, we randomly took some pairs of related concepts as positive examples and some pairs of unrelated concepts as negative examples. For each of the two concepts in a relation example, we randomly selected one description (phrase) out of all the descriptions it may have (including its fully specified name). We did so because a clinical phrase may not always be a fully specified name and the method should also be trained to work with alternate descriptions. Then the task of relation identification is: given the two descriptions of two concepts of particular types, determine whether they are related by a particular relation or not. We are not aware of any other work that has considered such a relation identification task for SNOMED CT.

3.2 Machine Learning Approach for the Task

For every kind of relation along with its types, we built a separate relation identifier. It may be noted that sometimes a presence of a relation can be identified simply by detecting overlap between the words in the two descriptions. For example, for the phrase (a) in Table 2, the word "pain" overlaps, hence "severe pain in the stomach" is a "pain". Similarly for the phrase (b), "neoplasm of right lower lobe of lung" is a "neoplasm of lung". However, this is not the case for many other relations. For example, the phrase (c) does not contain "stomach structure" which is its "finding site". Hence besides mere overlap, the relation identifier system should be able to use several other clues. In the previous example, it should know that "gastric" generally means related to "stomach structure". As it will be a formidable task to manually encode every piece of such knowledge, we use machine learning approach so that the system would automatically learn this kind of knowledge from training examples.

Another kind of knowledge a relation identifier would need is what words in the clinical phrase indicate what relations. For example, the word "in" in a disorder concept would usually indicate a "finding site" relation to a "body structure". The machine learning system is expected to also learn this kind of knowledge from training examples. In our experiments, we used a baseline for comparison that uses only the amount of overlap for identifying relations.

We decided to use Support Vector Machine (SVM; Cristianini and Shawe-Taylor, 2000) as our learning algorithm because it has been shown to work well with thousands of features and hence has been widely used in natural language processing tasks which often involve use of several thousand features, for example, words and their combinations. An additional advantage of SVM is that one can implicitly specify potentially infinite number of features without actually enumerating them by defining a similarity function between the examples, called a *kernel*. This is also known as the *kernel trick*. For our relation identification task, we designed a specific kernel to enable the SVM learner to learn the kinds of knowledge it needs to learn which were mentioned earlier. It also incorporates word overlap which is sometimes a good indication of a relation. The kernel is defined as follows. Let A and B be two examples. Let ${c_1}^A$ and ${c_2}^A$ be the descriptions of the first and the second concepts of the example A respectively. Similarly, let ${c_1}^B$ and ${c_2}^B$ be the descriptions of the first and the second concepts of the example B respectively. Then the kernel $K(,)$ between examples A and B is defined as:

$$K(A,B) = sim({c_1}^A, {c_1}^B) * sim({c_2}^A, {c_2}^B) + sim({c_1}^A, {c_2}^A) * sim({c_1}^B, {c_2}^B) \quad (1)$$

where, $sim(,)$ is the similarity function between any two descriptions (which are phrases). In our experiments, we defined similarity as the number of common words. We also tried defining it as the number of common word subsequences (Lodhi et al., 2002; Bunescu and Mooney, 2005), but it did not result in any gain in the performance. Note that the above is a well-defined kernel because products and summations of kernels are also well-defined kernels (Haussler, 1999). The kernel is normalized by dividing it by the square-root of $K(A, A) * K(B, B)$.

We now explain this kernel and what its implicit features are. The first term of the addition is a product of the number of common words between the first concepts of the two examples and the second concepts of the two examples. This essentially counts the number of common word pairs present in the two examples such that in each example the first word is present in the first concept and the second word is present in the second concept. For example, if both examples have "gastric" present in the first concept and "stomach" present in the second concept, then it will count "gastric,stomach" as a feature present in both the examples. Thus this kernel term implicitly captures pairs of words, one in each concept, as features. Based on these features, the learner may learn what combination of word pairs indicate a relation.

The second term simply treats the number of words overlapping between the two concepts of an example as a feature. The product then indicates how similar the two examples are along this feature. As was indicated earlier, overlap is an important feature because often the descriptions of the related concepts have overlap of words. In general, the two addition terms could be weighed differently, however, presently we did not experiment with different weights and we simply let SVM learn appropriate weights as part of its learning process.

4 Experiments

In this section we describe our experiments on the relation identification task for SNOMED CT relations.

4.1 Methodology

As was noted earlier, we formed our dataset utilizing the existing relations present in SNOMED CT. There are hundreds of different kinds relations present in SNOMED CT, some of them are more important than others (examples of some of the unimportant relations are "duplicate concept" and "inactive concept"). We report our results on the fourteen important and most frequent relations, each of which had more than ten thousand instances. The "is_a(procedure,procedure)" relation had the highest number of $93,925$ instances. Since we had enough examples to choose our training and test examples from, instead of doing standard cross-validation, we ran five folds and in each fold we randomly selected five thousand training and five thousand test examples. Training beyond five thousand examples would lead to memory problems, but as our learning curves showed, the learning would generally converge by five thousand training examples.

For each relation, positive examples for both training and testing were randomly selected without replacement as pairs of concepts for which the relation is known to exist. Then equal number of negative examples were randomly selected without replacement as pairs of concepts of the required types which are not related by that relation. There was no overlap between training and testing datasets. We employed SVM using the LibSVM package[3] along with the user-defined kernel as defined in the previous section.

We measured *precision* and *recall*. Precision is the percentage of correctly identified relations out of all the identified relations. Recall is the percentage of correctly identified relations out of all the relations present in the test set. The evaluation was done for the combined output of all the folds. SVM can also give the confidences for its classification decisions through Platt's method (Platt, 1999). We used these confidences to measure precision and recall at every confidence level and plotted precision-recall curves. We also measured the maximum *F-measure* across the precision-recall curves, where F-measure is the harmonic mean of precision can recall.

We compared our approach with a baseline method which only uses the amount of word overlap between the two concepts to identify a relation between them. It is not a learning-based approach. It outputs its confidence on a relation as the degree of overlap between the two concepts (i.e. the number of common words after normalization for word lengths). We call this baseline the *similarity baseline*. Note

[3]http://www.csie.ntu.edu.tw/~cjlin/libsvm/

that the similarity scores are already included as features in the kernel used in the learning approach.[4] Since there were equal number of positive and negative examples, the accuracy of a random classifier would be 50%.

4.2 Results and Discussion

Relation	Similarity Baseline (%)	Trained System (%)
associated_morphology(disorder, morphologic_abnormality)	66.67	83.29
causative_agent(disorder, substance)	82.94	90.87
finding_site(disorder, body_structure)	66.67	84.35
finding_site(finding, body_structure)	66.67	89.11
has_active_ingredient(product, substance)	85.92	91.34
is_a(body_structure, body_structure)	79.82	89.55
is_a(disorder, disorder)	78.18	84.55
is_a(finding, finding)	78.98	87.06
is_a(organism, organism)	66.67	79.23
is_a(procedure, procedure)	73.49	86.58
is_a(product, product)	67.48	86.27
is_a(substance, substance)	66.67	68.73
part_of(body_structure, body_structure)	66.67	89.13
procedure_site_direct(procedure, body_structure)	66.67	87.47

Table 2: Maximum F-measures over the precision-recall curves obtained by the similarity baseline and by the trained system for the most frequent SNOMED CT relations.

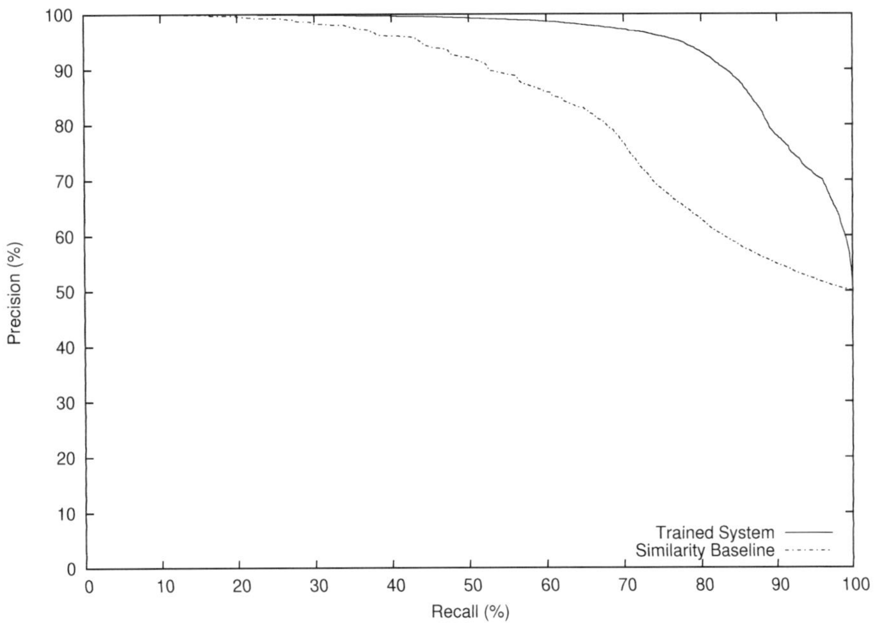

Figure 1: Precision-recall curves for the "is_a(procedure, procedure)" relation obtained using the similarity baseline and using the trained system.

Table 2 shows the maximum F-measures obtained across the precision-recall curves for the similarity

[4]We found that using the similarity score as the only feature in the learning method does not do well.

baseline and for the trained system for the fourteen most frequent relations in SNOMED CT. It may be first noted that the baseline does well on a few of the relations, obtaining close to 80% or more on five relations. This shows that the similarity baseline is not a trivial baseline although on some other relations it does not do well at all. Note that 66.67% F-measure can be also obtained by a random classifier by calling every relation as positive which would result in 50% precision and 100% recall. The learned approach does substantially better than the baseline on every relation. On eight of the fourteen relations it exceeds the baseline's performance by more than 10% (absolute). On five other relations it exceeds by more than 6%. The performance is close to 90% on five relations and is close to 80% or more on thirteen relations. The only relation on which the performance is not high is the "is_a(substance,substance)" relation. We found that this is mostly because a lot of new names are used for substances and from the names themselves it is not easy to identify that a particular substance is a type of another substance, for example, "lacto-n-tetrasylceramide, type 2 chain" is a "blood group antigen precursor".

Figure 1 shows the entire precision-recall curves obtained using the trained system and the similarity baseline for the "is_a(procedure, procedure)" relation. We are not showing these graphs for other relations due to space limitations, but this graph shows the typical curves obtained by the two methods. It may be noted looking at the lower part of the recall side that there are examples on which the relation can be identified with high precision even by the similarity baseline. But the learned approach continues to obtain high precision even on the high recall side when the precision of the baseline drops off. Finally, Figure 2 shows the learning curves for the same relation for the maximum F-measures on the precision-recall curves. Since the baseline method is not a learning method, its learning curve is horizontal. It can be seen that the learning method has almost converged and more training examples are unlikely to improve the performance substantially. It may also be noted that even with a few hundred training examples, the trained system already does much better than the baseline.

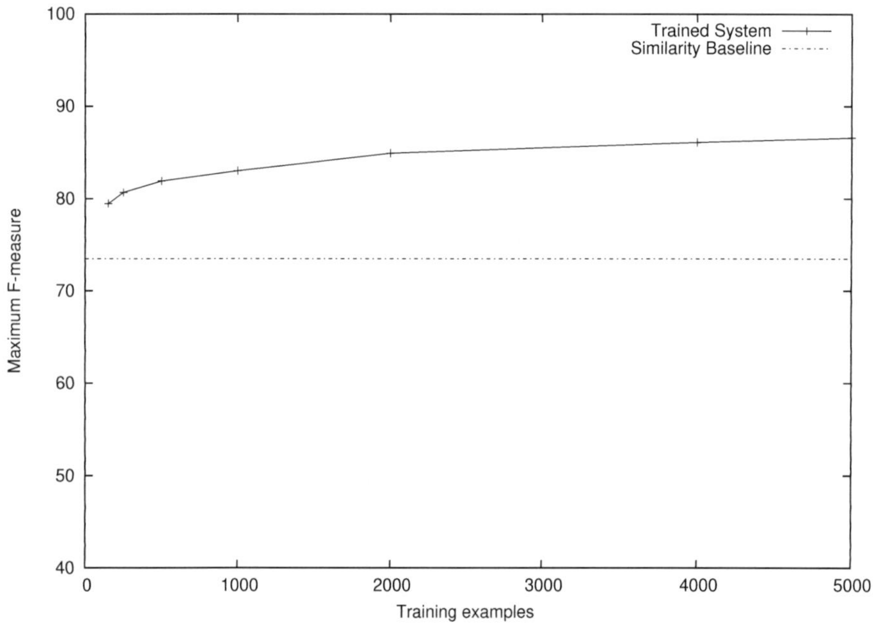

Figure 2: Learning curve for the "is_a(procedure, procedure)" relation obtained using the trained system. The similarity baseline is shown for comparison.

5 Future Work

There are several avenues for future work. Currently, our method does not do any syntactic analysis of the phrases. Clearly the syntactic structure of the phrase indicates the presence of relations with other concepts. Hence it will be potentially useful information to exploit. One may do this by using syntactic tree kernels (Collins and Duffy, 2001; Moschitti, 2006) for computing the similarity between the descriptions. Another way to improve the performance could be by incorporating the hierarchical structure of concepts in SNOMED CT as additional features. This may help the learner generalize across concepts at similar places in the hierarchy. In future, we also want to evaluate the performance of our method on clinical phrases which are not in SNOMED CT. This will, however, require manual evaluation by experts which may be doable only on a small scale.

In future, we plan to apply the SNOMED CT relation identification method to convert clinical phrases into their SNOMED CT expressions. We have already done some preliminary experiments towards this end. In order to identify relations for a new phrase, the system needs to check every relation with every other concept. Given that there are around four hundred thousand concepts in SNOMED CT, doing this is computationally very intensive (testing an example in SVM requires computing kernels with all the training examples which have non-zero support vectors). However, we tested the idea on a subset of SNOMED CT with around 3000 concepts whose all relations are preserved within the subset. We obtained maximum F-measures for the relation identification task in this setting in the range of $10 - 20\%$. But given that this test dataset contains a few thousand negative examples for every positive example (random guessing will perform less than 1%), this is in fact not a bad performance, although it needs to be improved. One way to improve will be to design a top level classifier that will filter out several obvious negative examples. Some of the SNOMED CT expressions require nested use of relations, for example, the expression for the phrase (d) in Table 1. In order to compositionally build a nested SNOMED CT expression, in future one may leverage ideas from semantic parsing (Mooney, 2007), the task of converting natural language utterances into complete meaning representations.

6 Conclusions

We formulated the task of identifying SNOMED CT relations as a means for converting natural language clinical phrases into SNOMED CT expressions. We presented a machine learning approach for identifying relations and also introduced an appropriate kernel for the task. Experimental results showed that the trained system obtains a good performance on the relation identification task.

References

Aronson, A. R. and F.-M. Lang (2010). An overview of MetaMap: Historical perspectives and recent advances. *Journal of the American Medical Informatics Association 17*, 229–236.

Baader, F., D. Calvanese, D. McGuinness, D. Nardi, and P. Patel-Schneider (2003). *The Description Logic Handbook: Theory, Implementation, Applications*. Cambridge, UK: Cambridge University Press.

Barrett, N., J. Weber-Jahnke, and V. Thai (2012). Automated clinical coding using semantic atoms and topology. In *Proceedings of Computer-Based Medical Systems (CBMS)*, pp. 1–6.

Benson, T. (2010). *Principles of Health Interoperability HL7 and SNOMED*. Springer.

Bunescu, R. C. and R. J. Mooney (2005). Subsequence kernels for relation extraction. In Y. Weiss, B. Schölkopf, and J. Platt (Eds.), *Advances in Neural Information Processing Systems 19 (NIPS 2006)*, Vancouver, BC.

Collins, M. and N. Duffy (2001). Convolution kernels for natural language. In *Proceedings of Neural Information Processing Systems (NIPS 14)*.

Cristianini, N. and J. Shawe-Taylor (2000). *An Introduction to Support Vector Machines and Other Kernel-based Learning Methods*. Cambridge University Press.

Friedman, C., P. O. Alderson, J. H. M. Austin, J. Cimino, and S. B. Johnson (1994). A general natural language text processor for clinical radiology. *Journal of the American Medical Informatics Association 2*, 161–174.

Friedman, C., J. Cimino, and S. Johnson (1993). A conceptual model for clinical radiology reports. In *Proceedings of the Seventeenth Annual Symposium on Computer Applications in Medical Care (SCAMC)*, pp. 829–833.

Friedman, C., L. Shagina, Y. Lussier, and G. Hripsack (2004). Automated encoding of clinical documents based on natural language processing. *Journal of Americal Medical Informatics Association 11(5)*, 392–402.

Haussler, D. (1999). Convolution kernels on discrete structures. Technical Report UCSC-CRL-99-10, UC Santa Cruz.

IHTSDO (2008). Compositional grammar for SNOMED CT expressions in HL7 version 3. External draft for trial use. Version 0.006, December 2008. Technical report, The International Health Terminology Standards Development Organization.

IHTSDO (2009). SNOMED Clinical Terms user guide. International release, July 2009. Technical report, The International Health Terminology Standards Development Organization.

Jung, S., S. Kim, S. Yoo, and Y. Choi (2009). Toward the automatic generation of the entry level CDA documents. *Journal of Korean Society of Medical Informatics 15(1)*, 141–151.

Lee, D. H., F. Y. Lau, and H. Quan (2010). A method for encoding clinical datasets with SNOMED CT. *BMC Medical Informatics and Decision Making 10:53*.

Lodhi, H., C. Saunders, J. Shawe-Taylor, N. Cristianini, and C. Watkins (2002). Text classification using string kernels. *Journal of Machine Learning Research 2*, 419–444.

Mooney, R. J. (2007). Learning for semantic parsing. In A. Gelbukh (Ed.), *Computational Linguistics and Intelligent Text Processing: Proceedings of the 8th International Conference, CICLing 2007, Mexico City*, pp. 311–324. Berlin: Springer Verlag.

Moschitti, A. (2006). Making tree kernels practical for natural language learning. In *Proceesings of the 11th Conference of the European Chapter of the Association for Computational Linguistics (EACL-06)*, Trento, Italy, pp. 113–120.

Platt, J. C. (1999). Probabilistic outputs for support vector machines and comparisons to regularized likelihood methods. In A. J. Smola, P. Bartlett, B. Schölkopf, and D. Schuurmans (Eds.), *Advances in Large Margin Classifiers*, pp. 185–208. MIT Press.

Sager, N., C. Friedman, and M. S. Lyman (1987). *Medical Language Processing: Computer Management of Narrative Data*. Reading, MA: Addison-Wesley.

Sager, N., M. Lyman, N. T. Nhan, and L. Tick (1995). Medical language processing: Applications to patient data representations and automatic encoding. *Methods of Information in Medicine 34:1/2*, 140–146.

Spyns, P. and J. L. Willems (1995). Dutch medical language processing: discussion of a prototype. In *Proceedings of the Eight World Congress on Medical Informatics*, pp. 37–40.

Spyns, P., P. Zweigenbaum, and J. L. Willems (1992). Representation and extraction of information from patient discharge summaries by means of natural language processing. In *Proceedings of MIC 92 (in Dutch)*, pp. 309–316.

Stenzhorn, H., E. Pacheco, P. Nohama, and S. Schulz (2009). Automatic mapping of clinical documentation to SNOMED CT. *Stud Health Technol Inform 150*, 228–232.

Uzuner, O., B. South, S. Shen, and S. DuVall (2011). 2010 i2b2/VA challenge on concepts, assertions, and relations in clinical text. *Journal of the American Medical Informatics Association 18*, 552–556.

Zelenko, D., C. Aone, and A. Richardella (2003). Kernel methods for relation extraction. *Journal of Machine Learning Research 3*, 1083–1106.

Zweigenbaum, P., B. Bachimont, J. Bouaud, J. Charlet, and J. F. Boisvieux (1995). A multilingual architecture for building a normalized conceptual representation from medical language. In *Proceedings of Ninth Annual Symposium on Computer Applications in Medical Care (SCAMC)*, pp. 357–361.

Analysis of Cross-Institutional Medication Information Annotations in Clinical Notes

Sunghwan Sohn[1], Cheryl Clark[2], Scott Halgrim[3], Sean Murphy[1], Siddhartha Jonnalagadda[1], Kavishwar Wagholikar[1], Stephen Wu[1], Christopher Chute[1], Hongfang Liu[1]
[1]Mayo Clinic, [2]MITRE, [3]Group Health Research Institute
{sohn.sunghwan, murphy.sean, siddhartha, wagholikar.kavishwar, wu.stephen, chute, liu.hongfang}@mayo.edu, cclark@mitre.org, halgrim.s@ghc.org

Abstract

A large amount of medication information resides in unstructured text in electronic medical records, which requires advanced techniques to be properly mined. In clinical notes, medication information follows certain semantic patterns (e.g., medication, dosage, frequency, mode, etc.). Some medication descriptions contain additional word(s) between medication attributes. Therefore, it is essential to understand the semantic patterns as well as the patterns of the context interspersed among them (i.e., context patterns) to effectively extract comprehensive medication information. In this paper we examined both semantic and context patterns and compared those found in Mayo Clinic and i2b2 challenge data. We found that some variations exist between the institutions but the dominant patterns are common.

1 Introduction

Electronic medical records (EMRs) have grown rapidly, and a large amount of clinical data is stored in free-text format. Natural language processing (NLP) techniques, which can convert unstructured text to a structured format, have been successfully applied in various clinical applications including patient medical status extraction [1, 2], sentiment analysis [3], decision support [4, 5], genome-wide association studies [6, 7], and diagnosis code assignment [8, 9].

Over the past decade, multiple clinical NLP systems have been developed and applied in the clinical domain, such as cTAKES [10], YTEX [11], MTERMS [12], HiTEXT [13], MedLEE [14]. Although clinical NLP systems have proven to be successful in many information extraction tasks, their performance often varies across institutions and sources of data [15, 16]. As some researchers have demonstrated, this may be due to the fact that clinical language is not homogeneous but instead consists of heterogeneous sublanguage characteristics [17-21].

Medication information is one of the major data components in EMRs. Patient medication history is of great concern for future medical treatments and plays a vital role in enabling the secondary use of EMRs for clinical and translational research. Although some medication information can be extracted from the structured data, a substantial amount of it resides in an EMR's unstructured text and requires advanced techniques, such as NLP, to extract. Since the medication information is described in various ways in the clinical notes, understanding the semantic patterns—i.e., description patterns of a medication name and attributes—and context patterns—i.e., context variations between the semantic patterns—is essential to effectively extract comprehensive medication information and develop a general and customizable medication extraction tool.

In this paper, we investigated both the semantic and context patterns of medication descriptions in clinical notes from two different sources: Mayo Clinic and the 2009 i2b2 medication extraction challenge [22]. We provide various pattern statistics and compare them at both the section level and the institution level to better understand the usage of semantic and context variations.

2 Background

Early research on medication extraction focused on extracting the medication name itself [23, 24] and mapping it to a standardized nomenclature [25]. The 2009 i2b2 medication extraction challenge focused on extracting comprehensive medication information (i.e., medication name as well as the attributes such as dosage, mode, frequency, duration, and reason) from clinical discharge summaries [22]. In this challenge, most top-performing teams used rule-based systems developed based on the examination of medication description patterns [22]. Because many of these systems performed well on most attributes, we may assume that medication information in clinical notes follows some patterns.

Some studies show that sublanguage-based clinical text processing systems, such as MedLEE [14], perform as accurately as medical experts on clinical concept extractions [13]. A sublanguage theory hypothesizes that the information content and structure from specific domains can be defined using a sublanguage grammar that specifies both domain-specific syntactic and semantic information [19, 26]. Aligned with sublanguage grammars, Xu et al. [27] performed a preliminary study on parsing medication sentences by assigning the probability to semantic-based grammar rules for medication detection. Their study showed promising results to disambiguate the complex sublanguage grammars of medication sentences.

Patterson and Hurdle [28] experimentally demonstrated that different clinical domains use their own sublanguages in clinical narratives. They conducted clinical document clustering in 17 different clinical domains and showed that note types in a broad clinical scope form the same cluster, but note types in a narrow clinical extent form different clusters. This study suggests that the performance of a clinical NLP system may depend on the source of the clinical notes and that the semantic and context information of the target notes should be seriously considered in the tool development process.

Previous studies support the idea that medication descriptions also exhibit sublanguage characteristics, and therefore an understanding of those characteristics in clinical notes within and across institutions is fundamental to properly extract medication information.

3 Materials and Methods

This study used annotated medication corpora from two sources: Mayo Clinic and the 2009 i2b2 medication extraction challenge data. The Mayo medication data consist of 159 clinical notes randomly selected from clinical notes. There are 659 manually annotated medication mentions with attributes. For i2b2 medication data, 253 discharge summaries from Partners Healthcare were manually annotated by challenge teams and released to the community for research [29]. In the combined corpora there are 9,003 medication mentions along with attributes. The semantic types of medication mentions and their abbreviations for both data sets are described in Table 1 (i2b2 annotations are excerpted from [29]).

We investigated both semantic and context patterns of medication descriptions in various aspects. The Mayo clinical notes consist of multiple sections explicitly separated by section tags. The i2b2 medication annotations include format information where the medication information is described—i.e., list vs. narrative. We included pattern variations within an individual section as well as a list vs. narrative format.

A. Semantic pattern parsing

The medication description in clinical notes consists of a medication name and its attributes such as dosage, frequency, mode, etc. We refer to a sequence of such semantics tags (ignoring other text between them) as the *medication semantic pattern*. For example,

	Aspirin was reduced to	1 tablet	po	twice	daily.	
Mayo:	m	do	fm	mo	fn	fu
	semantic pattern: *m|do|fm|mo|fn|fu*					
	Aspirin was reduced to	1 tablet	po	twice daily.		
i2b2:	m	do	mo	f		
	semantic pattern: *m|do|mo|f*					

We investigated these patterns in each data set and also compared them across the data sets (Mayo vs. i2b2). Since the two corpora have different annotation guidelines, we mapped semantically equivalent Mayo annotations to i2b2 annotations in the following way (Mayo → i2b2): mo → mo; sn, su, do → do; fn, fu →f; fm → N/A. In order to simplify the expression of semantic patterns we assigned a short symbol to dominant patterns. Table 2 contains those pairs and actual text examples.

TABLE 1. SEMANTIC TYPE ANNOTATION OF MEDICATION INFORMATION IN MAYO AND I2B2. PARENTHESIZED STRINGS IN THE SEMANTIC TYPE COLUMN ARE ABBREVIATIONS.

i2b2		Mayo	
Semantic type	**Definition**	**Semantic type**	**Definition**
medication (m)	medication name	medication (m)	medication name
dosage (do)	the amount of a single medication used in each administration (e.g., *"one tab" "4 units" "30 mg"*)	dosage (do)	how many of each medication the patient is taking (e.g., "2" in "2 daily", "*1*" in "1 tablet")
		strength number (sn)	e.g., "*30*" in "30 mg"
		strength unit (su)	e.g., "*mg*" in "30 mg"
frequency (f)	how often each dose of the medication should be taken (e.g., *"daily" "once a month" "3 times a day"*)	freq number (fn)	e.g., "*twice*" in "twice a day"
		freq unit (fu)	e.g., "*day*" in "twice a day"
mode (mo)	the route for administering the medication (e.g., *"oral" "intravenous" " topical"*)	route (mo)	same as the i2b2
duration (du)	how long the medication is to be administered (e.g., *"for a month" "during spring break"*)	duration (du)	same as the i2b2 but not include preposition (e.g., "*a month*" in "for a month)
		form† (fm)	the physical appearance of the medication (e.g., *aerosol, capsule, cream, tablet*)

†In i2b2, there is no form annotation but it may be part of the medication or dosage (e.g., m: "Aspirin tablet", do: "1 tab")

TABLE 2 EXAMPLES OF MEDICATION SEMANTIC PATTERNS AND SYMBOLS. IN EXAMPLE, SEMANTIC TYPES ARE ANNOTATED AS XML-STYLE TAGS.

<table>
<tr><th>symbol</th><th>semantic pattern</th><th>example</th></tr>
<tr><td>A</td><td>m</td><td><m>Aspirin</m></td></tr>
<tr><td>B</td><td>m|do|mo|f</td><td><m>Zocor</m> <do>5 mg</do> <mo>p.o.</mo> <f>q.h.s.</f></td></tr>
<tr><td>C</td><td>m|do|f</td><td><m>Glipizide</m> <do>5 mg</do> <f>b.i.d</f>.</td></tr>
<tr><td>D</td><td>m|mo</td><td><m>Lasix</m> <mo>drip</mo></td></tr>
<tr><td>E</td><td>m|do</td><td><m>Coumadin</m> <do>alternating doses of 4 mg</do></td></tr>
<tr><td>F</td><td>mo|m</td><td><mo>IV</mo> <m>ACE inhibitors</m></td></tr>
<tr><td>G</td><td>do|m</td><td><do>one unit</do> of <m>packed red cells</m></td></tr>
<tr><td>H</td><td>m|du</td><td><m>Dilantin</m> <du>for less than a year</du></td></tr>
<tr><td>I</td><td>m|f</td><td><m>Pepcid AC</m> <f>QHS</f></td></tr>
<tr><td>J</td><td>m|do|mo|f|du</td><td><m>KEFLEX (CEPHALEXIN)</m> <do>250 MG</do> <mo>PO</mo> <f>QID</f> <du>X 12 doses</du></td></tr>
<tr><td>K</td><td>m|do|mo</td><td><m>acetylsalicylic acid</m> <do>325 mg</do> <mo>p.o.</m></td></tr>
<tr><td>L</td><td>m|do|f|du</td><td><m>Lasix</m> <do>40 mg</do> <f>QD</f> <du>x3 doses</du></td></tr>
<tr><td>M</td><td>du|m</td><td><du>two days</du> of <m>Indocin</m></td></tr>
<tr><td>N</td><td>f|m</td><td>stable on <f>b.i.d.</f> <m>torsemide</m></td></tr>
<tr><td>O</td><td>m|mo|f</td><td><m>nitroglycerin</m> <mo>sublingual</m> <f>p.r.n.</f></td></tr>
<tr><td>P</td><td>m|mo|do|f</td><td><m>Lovenox</m> <mo>subcutaneously</mo> <do>90 mg</do> <f>daily</f></td></tr>
<tr><td>Q</td><td>do|mo|m</td><td><do>10 mg</do> of <mo>IV</mo> <m>Lopressor</m></td></tr>
<tr><td>R</td><td>mo|m|du</td><td><mo>IV</mo> <m>cefotaxime</m> <du>for the 7-day period</du></td></tr>
<tr><td>S</td><td>do|m|f</td><td><do>low dose</do> <m>dilaudid</m> <m>as needed</m></td></tr>
<tr><td>T</td><td>m|do|du</td><td><m>heparin</m> <do>500 units</do> <du>for 48 hours</du></td></tr>
</table>

B. Context pattern discovery

We use the phrase *medication context pattern* to refer to the semantic pattern plus the text that occurs between the semantic tags. Any text that occurs before the first semantic tag or after the last semantic tag is excluded. For example,

"The patient said that *Aspirin* was reduced to *1 tablet po twice daily* then stopped it"
Context pattern:
<m> was reduced to <do><mo><f> (i2b2)
<m> was reduced to <do><fm><mo><fn><fu> (Mayo)

C. Large corpus analysis (Mayo)

Mayo 159 clinical notes have a relatively lower number of medication descriptions (659 in Mayo vs. 9,003 in i2b2) and therefore it might cause sampling bias. To alleviate this issue we also examined 10,000 Mayo Clinic notes randomly selected from the Mayo patient cohort in the eMERGE study [30]. They were processed by the drug NER annotator in cTAKES [10] and their semantic patterns were parsed for comparison with i2b2. Drug NER uses rule-based pattern match implemented by finite state machine to parse medication and its attributes. These semantic patterns were not manually reviewed.

4 Results

A. Medication Semantic Patterns

1) Mayo data

In the Mayo corpus, there are a total of 89 unique semantic patterns, but 85% of the medication mentions occur in the 20 most frequent patterns; 70% of the medication mentions occur in the 5 most frequent patterns: *m* (322 mentions), *m|sn|su|fu* (85), *m|fu* (19), *m|sn|su|fn* (17), *m|sn|su|fn|fu* (16). Medication alone is the most dominant pattern, comprising almost half of all the medication mentions.

The Mayo clinical notes consist of multiple sections, and each section contains specific content. To further examine the content-based medication description, we analyzed each section separately and obtained section-specific semantic patterns. These results appear in Table 3.

TABLE 3. SECTION-LEVEL STATISTICS FOR MAYO MEDICATION SEMANTIC PATTERNS.

<table>
<tr><th>section</th><th># medications</th><th># patterns</th><th>patterns† (>=5)</th></tr>
<tr><td>Impression/Report/Plan</td><td>227</td><td>53</td><td>m (97), m|sn|su|fu (42), m|sn|su (8), m|fu (5),</td></tr>
<tr><td>Current Medications</td><td>183</td><td>38</td><td>m (52), m|sn|su|fu (28), m|fu (11), m|sn|su|mo|fu (9), m|sn|su|do|fu (9), m|sn|su|do|fn (8), m|sn|su|fn (6), m|sn|su (6), m|sn|su|fn|fu (5)</td></tr>
<tr><td>History of Present Illness</td><td>139</td><td>26</td><td>m (82), m|sn|su|fu (14), m|sn|su|fn (8), mo|m (5)</td></tr>
<tr><td>Allergies</td><td>39</td><td>1</td><td>m (39)</td></tr>
<tr><td>Past Medical/Surgical History</td><td>21</td><td>4</td><td>m (15)</td></tr>
<tr><td>Problem Oriented Hosp. Course</td><td>19</td><td>8</td><td>m (10)</td></tr>
<tr><td>Social History</td><td>10</td><td>3</td><td>m (8)</td></tr>
<tr><td>Chief Complaint/Reason for Visit</td><td>7</td><td>3</td><td>m (5)</td></tr>
<tr><td>The other sections</td><td>14</td><td>1</td><td>m (14)</td></tr>
</table>

†number within ( ) denotes # medications of a given pattern.

There are 14 sections that contain medications. Almost 90% of the medications appear in the four most dominant sections: Impression/Report/Plan, Current Medications, History of Present Illness, and Allergies. If we consider only patterns that occur five times or more throughout all sections, the Current Medication section is the most diverse with nine patterns. With the exception of the three most dominant sections, the other sections contain only one semantic pattern—*m (medication)*—that occurs five times or more. This pattern comprises all 39 mentions in the Allergies section.

2) i2b2 data

A similar dominance of a few patterns exists in the i2b2 corpus. Figure 1 shows the medication semantic patterns and their counts that cover 95% of the medication mentions in the 253 discharge summaries. A cumulative percentage denotes what portion of the counts from the total medication mentions appears in the given series of patterns up until that point. The semantic pattern in the figure is described as a short symbol with the actual semantic pattern in parentheses. There are a total of 69 unique semantic patterns, but 95% of the medication mentions occur in the 13 most frequent patterns.

3) Mayo vs. i2b2

In order to properly compare Mayo semantic patterns with i2b2 semantic patterns, the Mayo medication semantic tags were mapped to i2b2 tags. The distribution of these semantic patterns is presented in Figure 2. After mapping, 85% of the medication mentions occur in four dominant patterns *(m, m|do|f, m|do, m|do|mo|f)*, and 95% of them occur in 11 patterns.

Each i2b2 annotation also contains format information, indicating whether the mention occurred in a list or narrative context. Our observations of Mayo data show that the Current Medication and Allergies sections have a list format for the medication description, while the other sections have a narrative format. To compare the pattern variations in different formats, we characterized Mayo's Current Medication and Allergies sections as list and the others as narrative. As before, Mayo's semantic tag set was mapped to that of i2b2. The comparisons for list and narrative formats are shown in Figure 3 and Figure 4, respectively. The y-axis denotes the percentage of medication mentions out of the total medication mentions for a given pattern. We show the top 95% most frequent medication semantic patterns.

In list-formatted sections, Mayo data have five semantic patterns that cover 95% of the medication mentions while i2b2 data have nine (Figure 3). There are five semantic patterns that appear in both Mayo and i2b2. The most frequent pattern in the Mayo data is *"m"* while it is *"m|do|mo|f"* in the i2b2 data.

In the narrative sections, Mayo data have 13 semantic patterns that cover 95% of the medication mentions while i2b2 data have 15 (Figure 4). There are 10 common semantic patterns that appear in both the Mayo and i2b2 data.

To see the distribution of both Mayo and i2b2 semantic patterns in a larger data set, we also examined a large corpus of Mayo data. Ten thousand Mayo clinical notes were processed by the cTAKES drug NER module to annotate medication information, and we refer to the results as the Mayo 10K corpus. Note that these are system-generated results and were not manually reviewed by human experts.

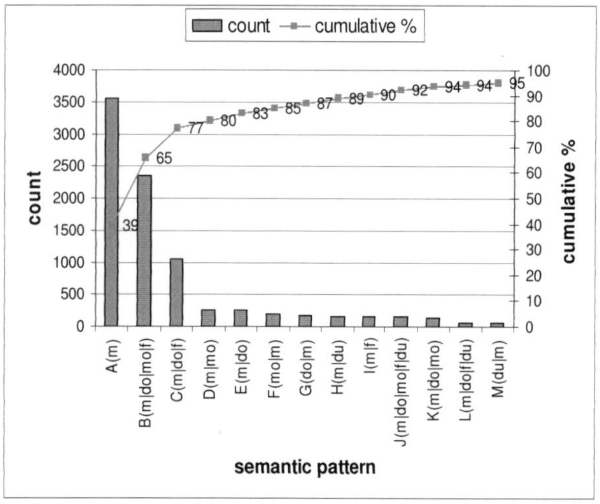

Figure 1. i2b2 medication semantic patterns (top 95%).

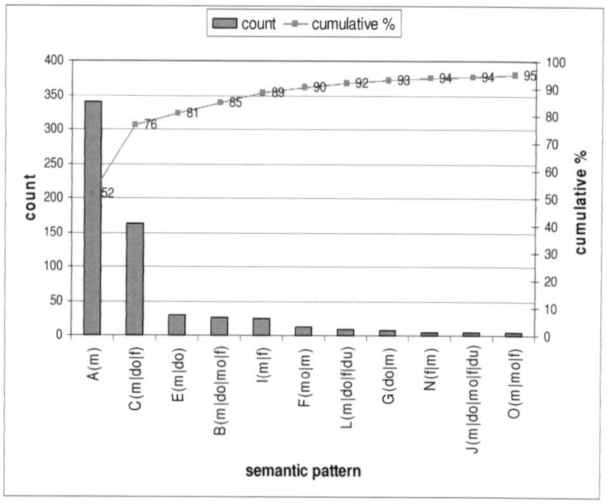

Figure 2. Mayo medication semantic patterns mapped to i2b2 (top 95%).

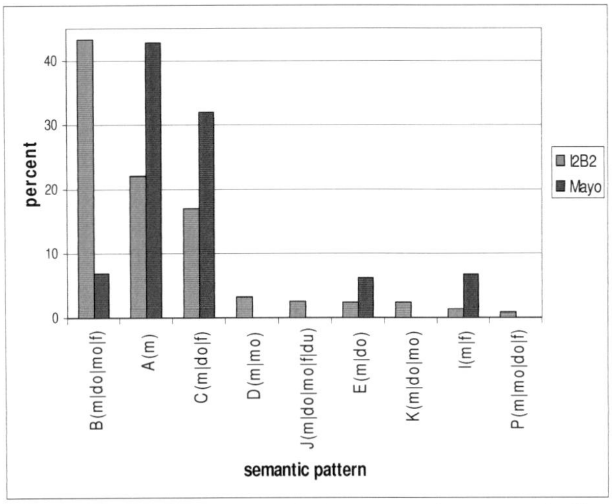

Figure 3. Mayo vs. i2b2 medication semantic patterns in list (top 95%).

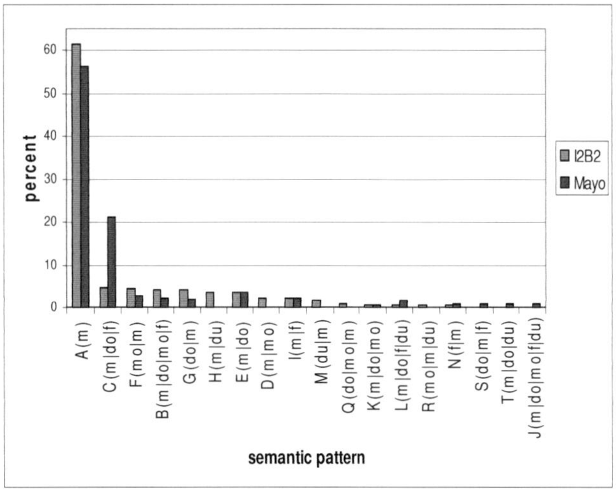

Figure 4. Mayo vs. i2b2 medication semantic patterns in narrative (top 95%).

Figure 5 shows the i2b2, Mayo, and Mayo 10K medication semantic patterns and also includes trends of those patterns (moving average with period two). The Mayo medication annotations were also mapped to the i2b2 annotations. In the top 95%, out of 15 semantic patterns, nine patterns appear in both Mayo and i2b2, four patterns appear only in i2b2 *(m|mo, m|du, m|do|mo, du|m)*, and two patterns appear only in Mayo *(f|m, m|mo|f)*. All data sets have the pattern of the medication name appearing alone as the most frequent pattern, but the second most frequent pattern in Mayo is *"m|do|f."* In both Mayo 10K and i2b2, it is *"m|do|mo|f,"* and this shows the notable difference in trends. In Mayo 10K, there is a total of 311,004 medication mentions, and 95% of all the medication mentions appears in nine sections. After mapping the Mayo annotations to i2b2, 95% of all the medication mentions occur in eight semantic patterns. Intriguingly, the Mayo 10K's three most dominant patterns *(m, m|do|mo|f, m|do|f)* exactly match with the three most dominant patterns of i2b2—they cover 80% and 77% of total medication mentions in Mayo 10K and i2b2 respectively. Comparing the trend to Mayo 159 notes, this larger Mayo corpus looks more similar to i2b2 semantic patterns.

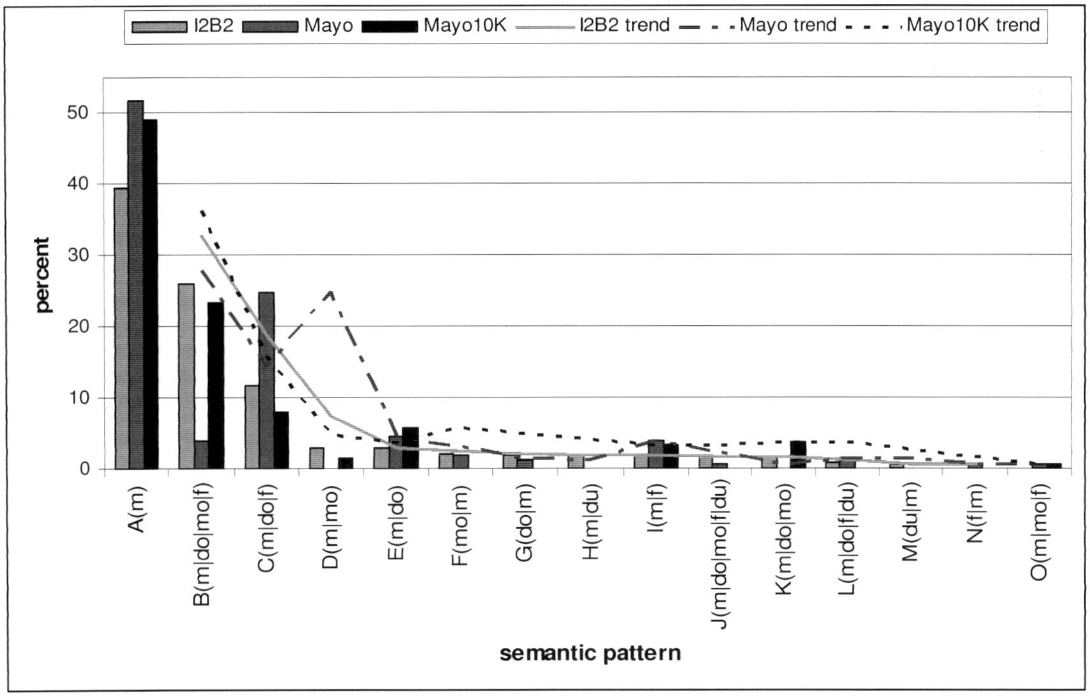

Figure 5. i2b2 vs. Mayo vs. Mayo10K medication semantic patterns with moving average trend (top 95%)

We also compared the semantic patterns in list vs. narrative for both data sets. In the list sections, Mayo's top three patterns *(m|do|mo|f, m, m|do|f)* also exactly matched the top three of i2b2, and covered 75% and 82% of the medication mentions in Mayo and i2b2, respectively. In the narrative sections, Mayo had only five patterns that covered 95% of the medication mentions, and all five patterns appeared in i2b2. Mayo's top two *(m, m|do|f)*, which covered 84% of the medication mentions, matched i2b2's top two patterns.

B. Medication Context Patterns

Medications in clinical notes are sometimes mentioned with additional words inserted between medication attributes. Those words may provide clues to medication semantics, so we examined this text.

1) Mayo data

The Mayo data have a total of 659 medication mentions. Out of those, only 93 cases (14%) have one or more words between medication semantic attributes. Of those 93 cases, 82 are unique. Since the individual words between the medication attributes are so varied, we did not notice a high frequency of exact context patterns. Therefore, we examined the semantic characteristics of the dominant partial context patterns. Table 4 shows statistics of dominant partial context patterns. When the medications are followed by verb forms, often the verbs are related to medication status changes—i.e., change of medication attributes. For example, *<m> was increased to <sn>*. The other minor patterns not in Table 4 are: *<m> another medication <fu>|<fn>*, x *<du>|<do>, <m> at <do>, <m> from <sn>, <m> be given <fu>, <m> were|used for <fm>*.

TABLE 4. MEDICATION CONTEXT PATTERNS IN MAYO (NUMBER DENOTES FREQUENCY)

<table>
<tr><th>Partial pattern</th><th>Status change pattern*</th></tr>
<tr><td>22 per|a <fu></td><td>6 <m> INCREASE indication <sn></td></tr>
<tr><td>12 for (period of|an additional) <du></td><td>1 <m> DECREASE indication <sn></td></tr>
<tr><td>7 <fn> times (a) <fu></td><td>3 <m> START indication <sn></td></tr>
<tr><td>6 <do>|<mo> every <fn></td><td></td></tr>
<tr><td>5 <m> dose|cycle (of|at) <sn></td><td></td></tr>
<tr><td>5 <m> to <sn></td><td></td></tr>
<tr><td>5 <su>|<du>|<fm> of <m></td><td></td></tr>
</table>

* Lexical variations were normalized

2) i2b2 data

Since i2b2 medication annotations are more coarse-grained than Mayo, we were able to find a high frequency of exact context patterns. In i2b2, there are a total of 9,003 medication mentions, and only 390 of those (4%) contain word(s) between medication attributes. Out of those 390 cases, 231 are unique context patterns. Table 5 shows the major exact and partial context patterns. Approximately one third of the total exact patterns belong to the exact patterns in Table 5. Similar to the Mayo data, when the medications are followed by verb forms, many are related to medication status changes. For example, *<m> was started...<du>, <m> was increased to <do>, <m> was reduced to <do>*. Another medication mention also appears between medication semantics, for example, *<m> and Lipitor <du>*. The other minor patterns include *<m> on <do>, <mo> with <m>*.

TABLE 5. MEDICATION CONTEXT PATTERNS IN I2B2 (NUMBER DENOTES FREQUENCY)

<table>
<tr><th>Exact pattern</th><th>Partial pattern</th><th>Status change pattern*</th></tr>
<tr><td>71 <do> of <m></td><td>141 <do>|<du> of <m></td><td>16 <m> INCREASE indication <do></td></tr>
<tr><td>28 <du> of <m></td><td>21 <m> at <do></td><td>2 <m> INCREASE indication <f></td></tr>
<tr><td>9 <do> of <m> <f></td><td>8 <m> (dose) from <do></td><td>1 <m><do> INCREASE indication <f></td></tr>
<tr><td>8 <du> of <mo> <m></td><td>5 <m> from <do></td><td>8 <m> DECREASE indication <do></td></tr>
<tr><td>6 <m> at <do></td><td>6 <m> to <do></td><td>1 <m> DECREASE indication <du></td></tr>
<tr><td>6 <do> of <mo> <m></td><td>4 <m> with <do></td><td>1 <m> DECREASE indication <f></td></tr>
<tr><td>5 <m> at <do> <mo> <f></td><td></td><td>8 <m> START indication <do></td></tr>
<tr><td>5 <m> at <do> <f></td><td></td><td>3 <m> START indication <du></td></tr>
<tr><td>5 <do> of <m> <du></td><td></td><td>1 <du> START indication <m></td></tr>
</table>

* Lexical variations were normalized

5 Discussion

Medication information was expressed in numerous ways in the clinical notes. We have investigated the medication description patterns in manually annotated data from 159 Mayo clinical notes and 253 i2b2 discharge summaries. Additionally, we have further compared these with a large medication corpus compiled by cTAKES drug NER from Mayo's 10,000 clinical notes.

Notes from Mayo and i2b2 share most of the common semantic patterns, but differences exist. Overall, the medication name alone is the most dominant pattern in both data sets. In Mayo, about 90% of the medication mentions occur in four sections, and all but the Allergies section contain a variety of semantic patterns. The Allergies and the other sections mostly contain the medication name alone.

In lists, i2b2 has *"m|do|mo|f"* as the most frequent pattern, but in Mayo data it is the medication name. This might be because Mayo's samples of 159 notes contain a relatively lower portion of Current Medication sections, which in fact, contain most of the medication information, as well as the most common list-format section. After mapping the Mayo annotations to the i2b2 annotations, the most frequent pattern in the Current Medication section is *"m|do|f."* Based on these observations, we could conclude that the list-format medication descriptions tend to provide at least the minimum information necessary to guide the proper medication intake (i.e., medication with dosage, frequency and possibly mode information).

In narratives, the pattern of the medication name alone is the most frequent in both data sets. Generally, narratives in clinical notes describe the physician's impression, report, and plan, as well as the patient's medical history, diagnosis, etc. In content of this nature, we may assume that physicians often simply mention medication names without further detailed attributes in clinical narratives as they are describing other conditions. The second dominant pattern in both data sets is *"m|do|f"*—21% and 5% out of the total medication mentions in Mayo and i2b2 respectively. In both data sets, the rest of the patterns cover a lower number of the medication mentions.

After mapping the Mayo annotations to i2b2, it can be seen that 12% (N=11) of the semantic patterns cover 95% of the medication mentions. In i2b2, 19% (N=13) of the semantic patterns cover 95% of the medication mentions. The i2b2 medication mentions are slightly more diverse than Mayo's. Covering 95% of the entire medication mentions from both data sets are total 15 semantic patterns, nine of which are common in both.

In both Mayo's 159 notes and i2b2, the medication descriptions do not contain many words between the medication attributes—14% and 4% of medication mentions contain some words between them in Mayo and i2b2, respectively. One reason for the higher context pattern for the Mayo data is due to different annotations. For example, if we look at duration, Mayo does not contain prepositions (e.g., for a week → duration is "a week") but i2b2 does (duration is "for a week"). Some prepositions like "of" are commonly used in combination with medication and dosage/duration (e.g. dosage or duration of medication). When a medication is followed by a verb, it can be related to a medication status change in many cases. Such medication status change descriptions often follow a pattern like: *medication + status change verb + dosage or frequency.*

When we examined a large Mayo corpus of 10,000 clinical notes, those semantic patterns were even closer to i2b2. Although there is more similarity between the two, Mayo 10,000 clinical notes have not been reviewed manually and therefore this might make the results slightly less reliable. The trends of i2b2 and Mayo 10K in Figure 5 seem to be very similar. The top three semantic patterns, which cover the majority of the medication mentions, are exactly matched with i2b2's. The portion of the list of medication descriptions is also closer to i2b2 than Mayo 159 notes. In Mayo 10K, 49% of the medication mentions belong to the list format (34% in Mayo 159 note); in i2b2, 56% belong to the list format. These observations imply that a medication extraction tool based on the semantic patterns in Mayo data may work reasonably well for i2b2 and vice versa.

In our semantic pattern analysis, we considered only one medication mention at a time. For example, "Aspirin or Tylenol 1 tablet prn" generates two instances of the semantic pattern *"m|do|f"* instead of *"m|m|do|f"*. In the future, we will further compile and analyze these kinds of patterns.

As shown in this study, the sublanguage of medication description in general can be well-characterized through semantic patterns. A medication extraction tool can utilize sublanguage—i.e., instantiating a given medication template with a given medication and the corresponding attributes. The statistics of medication patterns obtained in this study can be used as a confidence measure to determine whether a given medication and nearby attributes are truly associated or not. If its description pattern belongs to one of the majority patterns, we have high confidence in considering it as a correct association.

6 Conclusion

The semantic patterns that are used to describe medications vary in clinical notes as a whole, and some variations also exist between institutions. However, dominant patterns do exist that account for most of the medication descriptions, and most of those patterns are common between Mayo and i2b2. Extra context between the medication attributes is not common in the medication descriptions, but it does occur in some particular patterns primarily associated with medication, including the dosage or duration "of" medication and a medication followed by a status change verb. Those semantic and context patterns could be utilized to properly parse medication and its attributes, as well as to correctly associate them.

Acknowledgements

This manuscript was supported by Strategic Health IT Advanced Research Projects (SHARP) Program (90TR002), National Science Foundation ABI:0845523, and National Institute of Health 5R01LM009959. Jonnalagadda was supported by grant number 1K99LM011389 from the NLM.

References

1 Sohn S, Kocher J-PA, Chute CG, Savova GK. Drug side effect extraction from clinical narratives of psychiatry and psychology patients. J Am Med Inform Assoc. 2011;**18**(Suppl 1):144-9.

2 Sohn S, Savova GK. Mayo Clinic Smoking Status Classification System: Extensions and Improvements. AMIA Annual Symposium; 2009; San Francisco, CA: 619-623.

3 Sohn S, Torii M, Li D, Wagholikar K, Wu S, Liu H. A Hybrid Approach to Sentiment Sentence Classification in Suicide Notes. Biomedical informatics insights.**2012**(Suppl. 1):43-50.

4 Demner-Fushman D, Chapman W, McDonald C. What can natural language processing do for clinical decision support? Journal of Biomedical Informatics. 2009;**42**(5):760-72.

5 Aronsky D, Fiszman M, Chapman WW, Haug PJ. Combining decision support methodologies to diagnose pneumonia. 2001: American Medical Informatics Association; 2001. p. 12.

6 Kullo IJ, Fan J, Pathak J, Savova GK, Ali Z, Chute CG. Leveraging informatics for genetic studies: use of the electronic medical record to enable a genome-wide association study of peripheral arterial disease. Journal of the American Medical Informatics Association. 2010;**17**(5):568-74.

7 Kullo IJ, Ding K, Jouni H, Smith CY, Chute CG. A genome-wide association study of red blood cell traits using the electronic medical record. PLoS One. 2010;**5**(9):e13011.

8 Friedman C, Shagina L, Lussier Y, Hripcsak G. Automated encoding of clinical documents based on natural language processing. Journal of the American Medical Informatics Association. 2004;**11**(5):392.

9 Pakhomov SVS, Buntrock JD, Chute CG. Automating the assignment of diagnosis codes to patient encounters using example-based and machine learning techniques. Journal of the American Medical Informatics Association. 2006;**13**(5):516-25.

10 Savova G, Masanz J, Ogren P, et al. Mayo Clinical Text Analysis and Knowledge Extraction System (cTAKES): architecture, component evaluation and applications. J Am Med Inform Assoc. 2010;**17**(5):507-13.

11 YTEX - Yale cTAKES Extension.

12 Zhou L, Plasek JM, Mahoney LM, et al. Using Medical Text Extraction, Reasoning and Mapping System (MTERMS) to Process Medication Information in Outpatient Clinical Notes. American Medical Informatics Association; 2011. p. 1639.

13 Zeng Q, Goryachev S, Weiss S, Sordo M, Murphy S, Lazarus R. Extracting principal diagnosis, co-morbidity and smoking status for asthma research: evaluation of a natural language processing system. BMC Medical Informatics and Decision Making. 2006;**6**(1):30.

14 Friedman C, Alderson PO, Austin JH, Cimino JJ, Johnson SB. A general natural-language text processor for clinical radiology. J Am Med Inform Assoc. 1994 Mar-Apr;**1**(2):161-74.

15 Fan J, Prasad R, Yabut RM, et al. Part-of-speech tagging for clinical text: wall or bridge between institutions? ; American Medical Informatics Association; 2011. p. 382.

16 Wagholikar K, Torii M, Jonnalagadda S, Liu H. Feasibility of pooling annotated corpora for clinical concept extraction. Proceedings AMIA CRI 2012; San Francisco, CA.
17 Friedman C. A Broad Coverage Natural Language Processing System. American Medical Informatics Association Symposium; 2000. p. 270-4.
18 Stetson PD, Johnson SB, Scotch M, Hripcsak G. The sublanguage of cross-coverage. American Medical Informatics Association; 2002. p. 742.
19 Friedman C, Kra P, Rzhetsky A. Two biomedical sublanguages: a description based on the theories of Zellig Harris. Journal of Biomedical Informatics. 2002;**35**(4):222-35.
20 Harris ZS. A grammar of English on mathematical principles: Wiley New York:; 1982.
21 Harris ZS. A theory of language and information: a mathematical approach: Clarendon Press Oxford:; 1991.
22 Uzuner Ö, Solti I, Cadag E. Extracting medication information from clinical text. Journal of the American Medical Informatics Association. 2010;**17**(5):514-8.
23 Chhieng D, Day T, Gordon G, Hicks J. Use of natural language programming to extract medication from unstructured electronic medical records. 2007;. p. 908.
24 Sirohi E, Peissig P. Study of effect of drug lexicons on medication extraction from electronic medical records. 2005; p. 308-18.
25 Levin MA, Krol M, Doshi AM, Reich DL. Extraction and Mapping of drug Names from Free Text to a Standardized Nomenclature. Proc AMIA Ann Symposium; 2007; p. 438-42.
26 Harris ZS. The structure of science information. Journal of Biomedical Informatics. 2002;**35**(4):215-21.
27 Xu H, AbdelRahman S, Lu Y, Denny JC, Doan S. Applying Semantic-based Probabilistic Context-Free Grammar to Medical Language Processing-A Preliminary Study on Parsing Medication Sentences. Journal of Biomedical Informatics. 2011.
28 Patterson O, Hurdle JF. Document Clustering of Clinical Narratives: a Systematic Study of Clinical Sublanguages. American Medical Informatics Association; 2011. p. 1099.
29 Uzuner Ö, Solti I, Xia F, Cadag E. Community annotation experiment for ground truth generation for the i2b2 medication challenge. Journal of the American Medical Informatics Association. 2010;**17**(5):519-23.
30 McCarty C, Chisholm R, Chute C, et al. The eMERGE Network: a consortium of biorepositories linked to electronic medical records data for conducting genomic studies. BMC medical genomics. 2011;**4**(1):13.

The VeriClig Project: Extraction of Computer Interpretable Guidelines via Syntactic and Semantic Annotation

Camilo Thorne, Marco Montali, Diego Calvanese
KRDB Research Centre for Knowledge and Data
Piazza Domenicani 3, Bolzano, Italy
{cthorne,calvanese,montali}@inf.unibz.it

Elena Cardillo, Claudio Eccher
Fondazione Bruno Kessler
Via Sommarive 18, Povo, Italy
{cardillo,eccher}@fbk.eu

Abstract

We consider the problem of extracting formal process representations of the therapies defined by clinical guidelines, viz., *computer interpretable guidelines* (CIGs), based on UMLS and semantic and syntactic annotation. CIGs enable the application of formal methods (such as model checking, verification, conformance assessment) to the clinical domain. We argue that, while minimally structured, correspondences among clinical guideline syntax and discourse relations and clinical process constructs should however be exploited to successfully extract CIGs. We review work on current clinical syntactic and semantic annotation, pinpointing their limitations, and discuss a CIG extraction methodology based on recent efforts on business process modelling notation (BPMN) model extraction from natural language text.

1 Problem Description

Clinical guidelines are evidence-based documents compiling the best practices for the treatment of an illness or medical condition (e.g., lung cancer, flu or diabetes): they are regarded, following Shahar et al. (2004), as a major tool in improving the quality of medical care. More concretely, *they describe or define* the "ideal" (most successful) *care plans or therapies* healthcare professionals should follow when treating an "ideal" (i.e., average) patient for a given illness. Being general, guidelines need to be modified or instantiated relatively to available resources by health institutions, patients or doctors into protocols, and implemented thereafter into clinical workflows or *careflows* within clinical information systems. An important intermediate step for the synthesis of protocols and careflows from guidelines are *computer interpretable guidelines* (CIGs), viz., formal representations of the main control flow features of the described treatment and of its process or plan structure. CIGs can be exploited in a plethora of ways by clinical decision support systems to provide execution support and recommendations to the involved practitioners, guide the refinement into executable clinical protocols and careflows, and check for conformance and compliance.

Clinical document processing, and in particular the authoring of CIGs, protocols and careflows, is however a very costly and error prone task as it involves many layers of manual processing and annotation by experts. This explosion in costs, as pinpointed by Goth (2012), raises the need to develop biomedical NLP techniques, specifically: **(1)** clinical information extraction (IE) techniques and **(2)** automated CIG extraction methodologies.

The VeriClig project[1], a joint project involving the KRDB Research Centre for Knowledge and Data (Faculty of Computer Science, Free-University of Bozen-Bolzano) and the eHealth group from the Fondazione Bruno Kessler (Trento), intends to address the research problem **(2)** by adopting a computational semantics approach that aims at extracting CIGs from textual clinical guidelines. Our objective is to extract the main control-flow structures emerging from the textual description of guidelines in order to explore, in a second step, the possibility to express them using well-known representation languages.

[1] http://www.inf.unibz.it/~cathorne/vericlig

1.5.1.2 Emphasise advice on healthy balanced eating that is applicable to the general population when providing advice to people with type 2 diabetes.
1.5.1.3 Continue with metformin if blood glucose control remains inadequate and another oral glucose-lowering medication is added.

Figure 1: An excerpt from the NICE diabetes-2 clinical guideline[2]. Each line describes atomic treatments that combine together into a complex therapy.

One such language is the business processing modeling notation (BPMN) standard (see Ko et al. (2009)). Process specification and representation languages allow to leverage on formal methods (verification, model checking) as in Hommenrsom et al. (2008), which are useful for reasoning about the extracted CIGs and relate them with the corresponding executed clinical process. To realize our objective, we build on the work on clinical semantic and syntactic annotation mentioned above as well as on recent efforts on BPMN model extraction by Friederich et al. (2011).

2 Clinical Guidelines and Processes

Clinical guidelines such as, for instance, guidelines related to chronic diseases such as diabetes, allergies or lactose intolerance, are minimally structured documents. They possess however some crucial features: **(1)** they describe a *process*, generically intended as a set of coordinated activities, structured over time, to jointly reach a certain goal, and **(2)** the structure of the process they describe is significantly reflected by English *syntax* and *vocabulary*.

Processes. There are several ways to formally characterize processes, but little consensus as to which is the most appropriate for therapies. Thus, we do not intend at this stage to commit ourselves in the VERICLIG project to a particular formalism, but intend rather to focus on the main features such formalisms share, and in particular on their most basic, common constructs. For convenience, we use the terminology coming from the BPMN standard. In BPMN a process is a complex object constituted by the following basic components:

(*i*) *activities* (e.g., providing advice, controlling blood glucose levels), representing units of execution in the process;
(*ii*) participants, viz., the *actors* (e.g., doctors, nurses, patients), represented using pools, which are independent, autonomous points of execution, and possibly lanes, detailing participants belonging to the same pool;
(*iii*) *artifacts* or *resources* (e.g., metmorfin) used or consumed by activities;
(*iv*) *control flows and gates* (e.g., "if... then... else" control structures) that specify the acceptable orderings among activities inside a pool;
(*v*) *message flows*, representing information exchange between activities and participants belonging to different pools.

Process-evoking Categories. In English, *content words* provide the vocabulary of the domain, denoting the objects, sets and (non-logical) relations that hold therein; their meaning (denotation) is static. On the other hand, *function words* denote the logical constraints, relationships and operations holding over such sets and relations. This distinction holds also to some degree (as allowed by their inherent ambiguity) in clinical domain documents, giving way to *process-evoking word categories* (and constituents).

Figure 1 provides an excerpt taken from a diabetes guideline. In it, activities, actors and artifacts/resources (i.e., static information) are denoted by content words. Activities are denoted often by transitive, intransitive or ditransitive verbs, viz., **VB**s[3] and **VBZ**s, participles (**VBN**s), gerunds (**VBGs**),

[2] `http://www.nice.org.uk/nicemedia/pdf/CG87NICEGuideline.pdf`
[3] In what follows we refer to Penn Treebank word category and syntactic constituent tags, see Marcus et al. (1993).

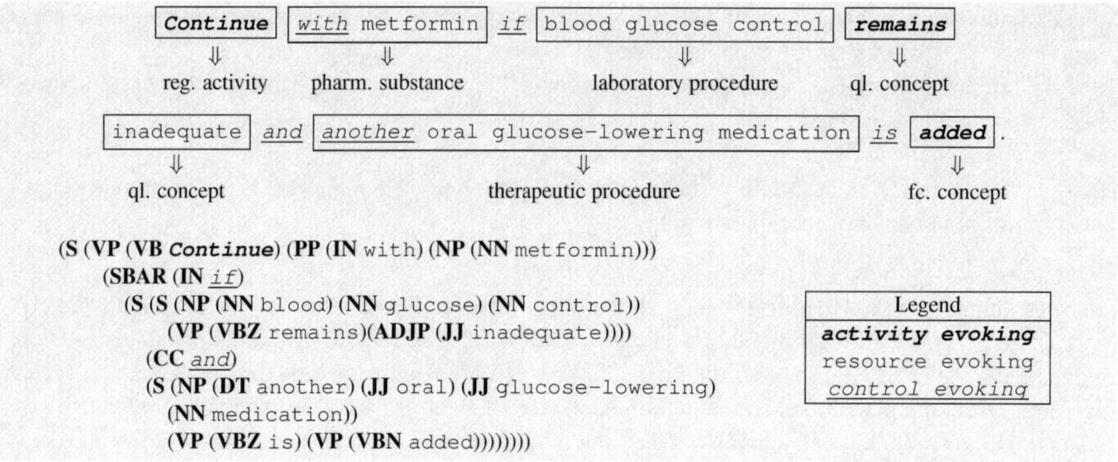

Figure 2: **Top:** MetaMap UMLS (automated) annotation of item 1.5.1.3 from Figure 1. Word highlighting is ours. Entity segmentation (boxes) and annotations are MetaMap's. **Bottom left:** Parse tree obtained with the Stanford parser. Word highlighting is ours.

etc, while actors and resources are denoted by the **NP** complements of such verbs. Control flows (i.e., dynamic, temporal information) are, on the other hand, denoted by function words, i.e., by **(a)** connectives introducing subordinated or coordinated phrases (e.g., **IN**s such as "if", in Figure 1), and **(b)** temporal adverbs (e.g., "following", in Figure 1) or prepositions (e.g., "after", in Figure 1). Such connectives and adverbs are called in NLP literature *discourse relations* since they are used to combine together phrases (noun and verb phrases) and sentences (whether main or subordinated). The correspondences among syntax, discourse relations and clinical process constructs should be exploited to successfully extract clinical processes.

3 Extraction of CIGs: Open Challenges

The main challenge in CIG extraction consists in how to combine semantic annotation techniques, focusing on content words (i.e., on entities and events), with syntactic annotation techniques capable of understanding the control flow structure conveyed by discourse relations, and information extraction methods dealing with clinical English ambiguity. In this section we provide an overview of the research challenges and of our proposed methodology to tackle them.

Limitations of Current Biomedical Resources. Research in biomedical NLP has yielded significant semantic annotation resources. Above all, the US National Library of Medicine's Unified Medical Language System (UMLS) Metathesaurus[4] and the annotated corpora, SemRep and annotation tools built upon it, MetaMap and SemRel, as described by Aronson and Lang (2010). MetaMap is used to map biomedical text to the UMLS Metathesaurus or, equivalently, to discover Metathesaurus concepts referred to in text. MetaMap uses a knowledge-intensive approach based on symbolic, NLP and computational linguistics techniques. Besides being applied for both IE and data-mining applications, MetaMap is one of the foundations of the US National Library of Medicine Medical Text Indexer (MTI) which is being used for both fully and semi automatic indexing of biomedical literature. Other resources that need to be mentioned are the semantically annotated CLEF corpus by Roberts et al. (2007), and Mayo Clinic's Java API cTAKES (version 2.5), by Savova et al. (2010).

Such resources, however, are still of limited use for the CIG extraction task. Gold-standard annotated guidelines are scarce for training and evaluation, and, if available, are not always in the public domain or might not support all biomedical IE tasks. Table 1 shows the main features of the mentioned biomedical

[4] http://www.nlm.nih.gov/research/umls/

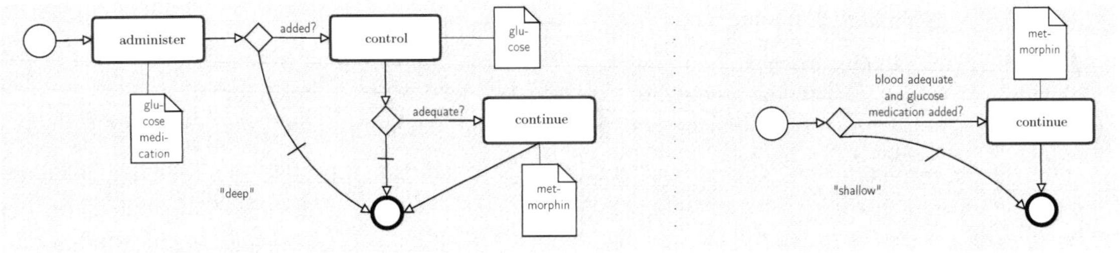

Figure 3: Two possible CIGs (in BPMN notation) of example 1.5.1.3 from Figure 1. Round boxes denote activities, diamonds conditional gates, square boxes resources and edges message flows. Circles represent the end (bold) and beginning of the process (normal), and barred edges "else" conditions.

Resource	ER	TE	RE	ANA	WSD	EV	Type	Open domain
CLEF	✓	✓	✓	✓	×	✓	Annotated corpus	×
UMLS	✓	✓	×	×	✓	×	Lexical resource	× (free for res.)
cTAKES 2.5	✓	✓	✓	✓	×	✓	Java API	✓
SemRep	✓	✓	✓	×	×	✓	Annotated corpus	× (free for res.)

Table 1: Main clinical and biomedical NLP resources and the features/IE tasks they support: entity recognition (ER), term extraction (TE), relation extraction (RE), anaphora resolution (ANA), word sense disambiguation (WSD) and event extraction (EV).

resources.

Crucially, bio-medical/clinical IE systems often overlook process control structure or improperly understand clinical documents. Figure 2 illustrates a SemRel/MetaMap UMLS annotation of example 1.5.1.3 from Figure 1, with its associated phrase structure parse tree. As the reader can see, such tools annotate only the identified "entities", viz., the verbs and **NP**s, overlooking process structure as conveyed by discourse relations. Alternative IE techniques applied to guidelines such as Kaiser et al. (2005) make extensive use of such resources. On the other hand, syntactic parsing, while necessary, as it can identify many discourse relations (e.g., the (**IN** `if`) constituent in Figure 2) and many of their arguments, is not sufficient, due to its limited domain knowledge: it provides little information regarding reified activities (e.g., the UMLS "procedures" in Figure 2). This may give rise to low precision, recall and accuracy for extraction methodologies based on either resource taken *alone*.

Research Steps. The VERICLIG project seeks to understand whether these limitations can be overcome using techniques coming from the business processing community. Friederich et al. (2011) showed how to mine control flow semantics from parse trees (phrase structure and typed dependency trees) computed from business policy documents to extract (generic) business processes in BPMN notation with reasonably high accuracy ($> 70\%$). We would like to adapt their general techniques to the clinical setting, by combining it with biomedical annotations.

For instance, to assign to example 1.5.1.3 the "deep" CIG representation (in BPMN notation) from Figure 3, which we believe accurately captures its semantics, and not the "shallow" one, we need to *combine* the output of syntactic and semantic annotation techniques. SemRep/MetaMap cannot extract process structure, but knows that "medication" and "control" (**NN**s) denote activities and not resources. Parsing, on the other hand, allows us to infer an "if...then...else" control structure, giving rise to the "shallow" process. However, by combining both sources of knowledge, we can see that the subordinated conditional phrase can be broken into a *sequence* of nested "if...then...else" structures. In addition to this, we need to provide support for ambiguity, temporal relations and anaphora resolution, as anaphoric dependencies and temporal relations are needed to build complex models that interconnect the process fragments extracted from each of the guideline's lines. As the reader may infer from Figure 3, process (and hence CIG) components temporally relate to each other, a feature spatially represented in BPMN's graphical notation; thus, we also need to extract such relations. These considerations give rise to the following CIG extraction methodology:

(*i*) combine annotation resources to extract CIG resources, actors and activities,
(*ii*) analyze syntactic/dependency structure to extract CIG control structure, and
(*iii*) resolve ambiguities and co-references, and infer temporal relations to build a complex CIG.

The work by Friederich et al. (2011) has the advantage, moreover, of proposing alternative methods for measuring, e.g., extraction accuracy, less dependent on the availability of Gold corpora, by comparing the similarity of the extracted model with that of the workflow implemented in business information systems. As both workflows and process representations or models (in, e.g., BPMN notation) are embeddable in graphs, an appropriate evaluation metric is *graph edit distance*. Given the availability of careflows in clinical information systems, this evaluation strategy should be applicable to our case.

In the near future, we intend to implement a baseline system to evaluate our proposed methodology along the lines discussed above. We are currently collecting a corpus of guidelines related to chronic diseases (e.g., diabetes, obesity, food allergy, etc.), and collaborating with local health institutions (the Merano hospital in Merano, Italy) to acquire the required careflows/clinical workflows for CIG extraction evaluation. To further refine CIG extraction, we will also consider applying formal methods (e.g., temporal logic reasoning) to prune logically inconsistent CIGs and/or their components.

References

Aronson, A. R. and F.-M. Lang (2010). And overview of MetaMap: Historical perspective and recent advances. *J. of the American Medical Informatics Association 17*(3), 229–236.

Friederich, F., J. Mendling, and F. Puhlmann (2011). Process model generation from natural language text. In *Proc. of the 23rd Int. Conf. on Adv. Inf. Sys. Eng. (CAiSE 2011).*

Goth, G. (2012). Analyzing medical data. *Comm. of the ACM 55*(6), 13–15.

Hommenrsom, A., P. Groot, M. Balser, and P. Lucas (2008). Formal methods for verification of clinical practice guidelines. In A. T. T. et al. (Ed.), *Computer-based Medical Guidelines and Protocols: A Primer and Current Trends*, Chapter 4, pp. 63–80. IOS Press.

Kaiser, K., C. Akkaya, and S. Miksch (2005). Gaining process information from cinical practice guidelines using information extraction. In *Proc. of the 10th Int. Conf. on Art. Int. on Med. (AIME 2005).*

Ko, R. K., S. S. Lee, and E. W. Lee (2009). Business process mangament (BPM) standards: A survey. *Business Process Management Journal 15*(5), 744–791.

Marcus, M. P., B. Santorini, and M. A. Marcinkiewicz (1993). Building a large annotated corpus of English: The Penn treebank. *Computational Linguistics 19*(2), 313–330.

Roberts, A., R. Gaizaskas, M. Hepple, N. Davis, G. Demetriou, Y. Guo, J. Kola, I. Roberts, A. Setzer, A. Tapuria, and B. Wheeldin (2007). The CLEF corpus: Semantic annotation of a clinical text. In *Proc. of the AMIA 2007 Ann. Symp.*

Savova, G. K., J. J. Masanz, P. V. Ogren, J. Zheng, S. Sohn, K. C. Kipper-Schuler, and C. G. Chute (2010). Mayo clinical text analysis and knowledge extraction system (cTAKES): Architecture, component evaluation and applications. *J. of the American Medical Informatics Association 17*(5), 507–513.

Shahar, Y., O. Young, E. Shalom, M. Glaperin, A. Mayafitt, R. Moskovitch, and A. Hessing (2004). A framework for a distributed, hybrid, multiple-ontology clinical-guideline library and automated guideline-support tools. *J. of Biomedical Informatics 37*(5), 325–344.